WALL STREET MONEY MACHINE

VOLUME 2

STOCK MARKET MIRACLES

You have to know your exit before ever going in the entrance.

—WADE B. COOK

WALL STREET MONEY MACHINE

VOLUME 2
STOCK MARKET MIRACLES

WADE B. COOK

Lighthouse Publishing Group, Inc.
Seattle, Washington

Lighthouse Publishing Group, Inc.
Copyright © 2000 Wade B. Cook

Library of Congress Cataloging-in-Publication Data
Cook, Wade.
Wall street money machine, volume 2, Stock market miracles / Wade B. Cook
p. cm.
Includes bibliographical references and index.
ISBN 1-892008-64-5
1. Speculation. 2. Stocks. 3. Futures. I. Title.
xoxoxoxoxoxoxoxox
xoxoxoxoxoxoxoxox   xoxoxoxoxoxoxo
CIP

"This publication is designed to provide general information in regard to the subject matter covered. It is sold with the understanding that the publisher is not engaged in rendering legal, accounting, or other professional services. If legal, accounting, or other professional services are required, the services of an independent professional should be sought."

"From a declaration of principles jointly adopted by a committee of the American Bar Association and the committee of the Publisher's Association."

Book Design by Judy Burkhalter
Dust Jacket Design by Angela Wilson
Dust Jacket and Inside Photographs by Zachary Cherry

Published by Lighthouse Publishing Group, Inc.
14675 Interurban Avenue South
Seattle, Washington 98168-4664
1-800-706-8657
206-901-3100 (fax)

Source Code: WSMMV200

Printed in United States of America
10 9 8 7 6 5 4 3 2 1

To Helene and Carl Cook,
My Mom and Dad

They raised me to appreciate life,
to live with passion,
to live by the rules,
and to help others.

CONTENTS

Preface   *ix*
Acknowledgments   *xiii*
What Participants Are Saying   *xv*

CHAPTERS

1   Building A Great Portfolio   1

2   Treat It As A Business   23

3   Earning Money   45

4   Quick Turn Profits   59

5   Fun-Damentals   73

6   Optimum Options   87

7   The Put-ting Green   99

8   How To Get A Free Ride . . . Sort Of   119

9   Knowing When To Sell   133

10   Selling Puts (My Favorite Strategy)   149

11   Option Exit Strategies On Stock Splits   163

12   Tandem Plays   179

APPENDICES

1   Behind Closed Doors   195

2   Available Resources   215

     Glossary   229

PREFACE

When I finished my last book, *Wall Street Money Machine, Volume 1*, I thought I had written everything I could write about my strategies for investing in the stock market. Then several things happened.

The first was a dramatic increase in our seminar business. This drove me to create, develop, try, and perfect new methods for portfolio cash flow enhancement–big words for getting more income out of investments, and using the excess cash flow to buy really good "keeper" stocks.

The second was, and I hope will continue to be, my thirst for knowledge–especially knowledge and wisdom which work in the marketplace. Fine tuning and getting bigger, better, and quicker returns, using stocks and purchasing variations to really generate a lot of income are major motivating factors in my life.

This second point leads to my third and final point. I want to be one of the very best educators in America. I do deals and learn so I can teach. I'm more into how a certain formula can be duplicated and then shared with others than into money for money's sake. I have a lot of money, and while that's nice, my real passion is helping others improve their lives.

This passion has me constantly searching, questioning, and visiting with others to figure out their real needs. I wrote this book to address those problems and concerns.

Right now, I'm sitting in an airport. I do a lot of that as I travel the width and breadth of this country helping people learn how to work the market. The balance of this book has been written and it is almost time to go to press. It's high time I wrote the preface so it will not hold up the process!

Why, you might ask, am I writing the preface last? Shouldn't it be done first to give direction to the book's plot? Maybe for some authors, but not for me. Not this time.

You see, I believe in serendipity. If you've read my first book on cash flowing formulas (*Wall Street Money Machine, Volume 1*), then you know how my system works. I have some ideas, and then I try to test them until I find one that works repetitiously. I guide my efforts to find new ways. Serendipity, to me, means a happy or joyous discovery on the way to something else. A dictionary defines it as such: "The faculty of making fortunate discoveries by accident."

As I tried new ways and perfected old ones, I wrote. Month after month I wrote and here's the book—a collection of new formulas, variations on old ones, and the rationalization and reasoning behind them. This turned out to be the book I wish I had written first.

This book was first published under the title *Stock Market Miracles*. Why the weird title? After all, there are not really miracles in the stock market. Perhaps miracles happen on 34th Street, but not on Wall Street. However, the returns these strategies create seem like miracles.

A miracle is a phenomenon that defies explanation. We usually think of miracles in a spiritual way, so let me go there and then segue my way back and show how this title came to be.

The Bible is the basis for the following: God intervenes in the lives of mortals. Sometimes what happens can't be explained. There is no rational explanation. I know there are pure miracles, but sometimes I wonder if God uses ordinary things like people, events, nature, et cetera to bring about good things. A grocery sack of food left on someone's doorstep could be a miracle and an answer to someone's prayer. A wise teacher, a passage of scripture, and a good friend could all provide many mini-miracles.

I have been able to obtain fantastic returns on so many stock market plays: 26,000% annualized one hour returns; 10,680% annualized in two days and so many more.

To some, these seem to defy logic, or at least they defy explanation. Not to me. They make sense. I do them often and so will you. These trades are sort of like a magic trick. At first it seems "stupendous"–other worldly. But as you learn the trick you say, "It's a piece of cake."

They are, however, miracles to some people because of what they are able to do in their own lives. I love attending our Wall Street Workshops™. Some people shake my hand so hard it takes a while to recover. People who needed $30,000 in four weeks to adopt three Cambodian babies had it four weeks after the class; a man who can spend (and has done so for over a year) $2,000 a month to help his mother, who is seventy-eight years old, retire better; another man with $30,000 who made $700,000 in about five months. Countless hundreds of people have retired on $7,000 to $15,000 per month, in less than six months, starting with usually around $5,000. The changes are real. They are not real miracles, but they have the same effect and the same impact.

If the returns you receive from implementing the following strategies seem to defy gravity, then great for you. You keep the profits. I get the satisfaction of knowing you're doing well.

I want to change the way you think. Read what was in the January 1st issue of *Forbes* Magazine 60 years ago: "Optimism is a tonic. Pessimism is poison. Admittedly, every businessman must be realistic. He must gather facts, analyze them candidly, and strive to draw logical conclusions, whether favorable or unfavorable. He must not engage in self-delusion. He must not view everything through rose-colored glasses. Granting this, the incontestable truth is that America has been built up by optimists. Not by pessimists, but by men possessing courage, confidence in the nation's destiny, by men willing to adventure, to shoulder risks terrifying to the timid." I am sure my dedication to excel and my passion for sharing will have us meet one day. I am a millionaire-maker. Our meeting will probably be at one of my training sessions. I wish you well as you stun and amaze those around you with these simple, yet effective, cash flow strategies. I live my life by and wholeheartedly agree with Albert Einstein's statement: "Many times a day I realize how much my own life is built upon the labors of my fellowmen, and how earnestly I must exert myself in order to give in return as much as I have received."

*Great spirits have always had violent opposition from
mediocre minds.*

—ALBERT EINSTEIN

ACKNOWLEDGMENTS

This book is not the product of studies or schoolroom research, but of live, active, try-it-till-it-works, in-the-trenches formulas and techniques. Students in the past have appreciated strategies that really work–simple, yet powerful–in that they produce results. I would like to acknowledge and give a heartfelt thanks to those on my staff whose dedication it is to help others. David McKinlay, Rich Simmons, Richard Lowman, George Park, Greg Harrop, Terry Cummings, Barry Collette, Todd Doyle, Eric Delahanty, and Sharon Armstrong on my research/trading and Wealth Information Network™ (W.I.N.™) have played important roles. My Wall Street Workshop™ instructors and technicians get kudos for their everyday work. To name a few: Linda Woolf, Freddie Rick, Rick Moore, Keven Hart, and Jay Harris. My gratefulness also extends to my students who wrote, faxed, and emailed me deals and strategies they use. The staff at Lighthouse Publishing–Brent Magarrell, and Judy Burkhalter–has rendered tireless service to bring these manuscripts to fruition. They carefully proof and create these books and deserve many thanks. To my department heads at Stock Market Institute of Learning who filled in and do such a great job as I take time out to write and travel: Carl Sanders, Carla Norris, Cindy Britten, Debbie Losse, Kathy Voorhees, Rick Smith, Robert Hondel, Robin Anderson, and so many others. My wife, Laura has been my sounding board and friend.

To all who have been a part, thanks!

WHAT PARTICIPANTS ARE SAYING

The following pages contain just a few of the testimonials we receive from our students. Your results will vary.

As an adult educator with a graduate degree in education as well as an M.B.A., I have found the three days of the Wall Street Workshop™ fast paced with information I have not found elsewhere—a real mind trip. 15 years as a self-employed businessman and in three days I multiplied my business knowledge many fold. Thanks.

—STEFAN G.

You have shown me how to generate my retirement income. In the last half of this year, I generated $70,000.

—JIM N.

When Wade said 'This course can cost you $100,000 if you don't go,' he was right. I bought a whole bunch of Fannie Mae calls on a Friday at ¹/4 and sold them the next Monday at ³/4. That's 200% in just a few days. Thanks Wade.

—GREG G.

In the past year, my IRA account increased by 84%, my wife's by 132%. My Nevada corporation earned $30,000 in its first year in business, not to mention what it saved in state income taxes. Obviously, I'm sold.

—KEN W.

I've learned many ways to help my portfolio in this seminar. I've done many covered calls and in one month made $15,000 to $16,000. Wade helped change my way of investing.

—CLIFTON F.

This has been an exciting two weeks for me and my family. It has been two weeks since I attended that Wall Street Workshop™. I can't begin to tell you the amount of electricity and confidence that is generated around my home recently. Before the workshop, I considered myself an average stock trader, at times performing fairly well, but otherwise just treading water. I have never had any formal training in the stock market, and after listening to most others (including brokers), I considered the option market strictly a "voodoo curse" to be wary of.

In your workshop, the second day of class I made my first two rolling options purchases. To my pleasant surprise, I was able to sell both options the following morning for a profit large enough to cover the complete cost of the workshop.

At home, after the excitement of the workshop, I began buying options as we were taught in class. So far I have used only one investment strategy (buying options on rolling stocks) and have completed 10 buys and sells. In the last 15 days I have been able to obtain a clear net profit of $23,252.35, after commissions. Yes, that's right! 74.4% in 15 days! I'm still pinching myself to see if I'm awake.

—MICHAEL K.

Wall Street Workshop™ flash: We made $3,100 in about six hours with the information taught in this workshop. Mike took this workshop in mid-January and made $35,000 in two months using rolling stocks and covered calls. The class was fabulous, the instructors were terrific, and we're coming out for the advanced workshop to learn even more. Thanks a lot.

—MIKE AND PAT O.

I love this stuff. I made a 27% profit on my money in less than 5 weeks! I can't wait till tomorrow to do it again.

—ROBERT G.

I finally understand options! I gained enough courage [at the seminar] to write some covered calls for a total profit of 78%.

—J.J.

I fully understand the benefits of covered calls, stock splits, rolling stocks, and options. It has been beneficial for me to be here. When Wade was speaking he was moving at a pace I could understand and implement.

—DONALD S.

This has been a very intense, but very informative workshop. I took advantage of this learning experience to get my feet wet in the securities market with a small investment and made $600. This has definitely been worthwhile.

—STANLEY N.

I heard about this seminar from my husband–he bought the tape series and made me listen to them. They were great! This seminar helped us to see that dealing with the stock market is something that we can do–as long as we do the research first.

—DANA T.

I knew nothing, nada, zilch about stocks when I met Wade; now, after the Wall Street Workshop™, I understand what to look for a lot better. The strategies and formulas will be very helpful for creating cash flow, which is why I came, and I thank you for teaching me. I will not give up (or quit bugging you guys) until I master them, especially rolling stocks and options.

I delivered pizzas all through college, and I quickly figured out that no matter what I did, I was averaging $1/run; therefore, *like Wade, I was doubling and tripling the amount everyone else was making waiting around on the 'big' tips. I really, really click with Wade's thinking–I love the meter drop mentality. I've been singing it all along; I just didn't know what to call it or where to use it. Obviously, that philosophy will pay much larger dividends (pun intended) in stocks than pizza delivery. Thanks Wade and Team!*

–JACKIE L.

My understanding of the stock market rose from $1^1/8$ to $102^1/4$.
–JOE O.

This seminar gave me an understanding of stocks and options that I could not have gotten elsewhere. The days of my losing money on deals I don't know or completely understand are over! Now I know how to make excellent returns and minimize my risk! I am excited and looking forward to managing my portfolio correctly–for the first time!

–SCOTT S.

My wife and I can now see a future where we are working together from home and being very successful. I will be doing this on a full-time basis and our goal is to have my wife out of work in 3 to 5 years. We earned $2,500 in our first two days of trading and we never traded in the stock market before. The experience has given us the opportunity to make a fortune, help our family, and live the kind of life we always dreamed of. Our dreams will become a reality thanks to Wade and his great staff, and we are only 32 and 31 years old!

–LEO K.

The following are participant comments on the Next Step™ advanced Wall Street Workshop™ seminar.

[The Next Step] added to the strategies presented in the Wall Street Workshop™. Gaps and Split strategies added new greatness to the trading of my stocks. It opened my eyes to playing the market on the upward and downward trends in the market. I better understand the put strategies and the straddle plays.

—JAY R.

I was worrying if the seminar would be worth the price. After 30 minutes of the first day, I knew I had already received more value than the price. The value increased by the minute thereafter. Thank you for a great seminar.

—ROBERT P.

[I attended my] first Wall Street Workshop™ in Houston, September 22-23. I started with $50,000 and my account is now at $177,000. Not "perfect," but I consider myself still on the learning curve. That is why I attended the Next Step™. I intend to place another $250,000 into play in the next two months. I started my first corporation, living trust, and limited partnerships two weeks ago. Six other people have attended the Wall Street Workshop™ at my urging and are making bucks already. All of this in six months!

—LANCE B.

I invested $5,000 in rolling USRX, in two days I made $4,750. In one day [with SWK] I made $1,875 and I turned a covered call with ASFT and made $3,500 in two days (for a total net profit of $9,625). The only thing I can say is: 'Thank you!'

—JIM C.

Call 1-800-872-7411 for more information about these courses.

1

BUILDING A GREAT PORTFOLIO

When my first book on stock market investing hit the street, I was overwhelmed by the incredibly favorable response. I received countless letters and email messages. These were no ordinary "thank yous," as most had included specific trades they had made, records of deals, and cash flow profits to be proud of. *"I've made $43,000 in one month," "$19,000 in three days," "We just adopted kids with the $30,000 we made this month."* Too many wonderful stories to mention here. See the testimonials at the beginning of the book for a sampling of the many exciting stories we hear.

There have been critics also. Don't misunderstand. I've not been criticized by anyone who actually read the book, and surely not by anyone who has followed the formulas and done the trades. Actually, the only real criticism has come from comments made on the jacket, like *"outrageous returns,"* or *"double your money every $2^1/2$ to 4 months."*

USING OPTIONS TO BUILD A PORTFOLIO

So to answer this light and superfluous charge, I dedicate this chapter to building a strong portfolio for the long term. I won't turn my back on my cash flow formulas. In fact, I'll use them to build a portfolio to be proud of—an "investment club" style portfolio, but I'll do so my way; defining the methods and even the terms, such as "long term."

I am no different than most prudent investors or pension and mutual fund managers. I want to look at my portfolio and see huge, brand name stocks like AT&T, Boeing, Wrigley, McDonalds, Nordstrom, Sears, General Electric, Pfizer, Marriott, et cetera. I want to own stock in companies I can eat in, shop at, dial up, and sleep in! I like quality. I repeat, I like great companies with excellent growth, trademarks, earnings, market niche, and sheer strength of size. I want millions of dollars of them and I don't want to have to work a 9 to 5 job to get them. Boy, that's a conundrum. It's almost impossible to work a typical American job with average income and accumulate millions. Yes, in 40 to 50 years maybe, but who wants to wait that long? That's the rub–accomplishing the task of having millions without having to work for millions. So, it is not my *goal* or objective which differs from the "conventional wisdom" reeking from virtually every financial planner/stockbroker–the so-called experts–but the *method* of getting there. This is where we part ways.

You see, my method is simple. I want to use a small amount of money–risk capital if you will–to generate cash flow that will exponentially generate more income. I've never advocated that a person put his entire portfolio at risk with aggressive plays. In fact I've repeatedly and strongly advised against it.

To prove this point, and so there is no misunderstanding, I'll repeat it here. Use a small amount of money–say $2,000 to $10,000–to build a cash flow machine. Keep the balance of your money in high-grade stocks, bonds, mutual funds, and even in real estate and other businesses outside the traditional stock market investments. The stock market is simply too risky for me.

Will Rogers said it best: "I'm worried about the return *of* my money, not just the return *on* it."

Let's deal with the $2,000 to $10,000 figures. That may seem high to participants of the "meet the 2nd Tuesday of each month, invest $50 a month and sit around for hours discussing one or two stocks and hope for the best" clubs so prevalent today. Let's break everyone into categories: those with *under $100,000* to invest, and those with *over $100,000* to invest. Everyone reading this falls into one of these two categories. That's simple, but the next part is not so simple. If you only have $2,000 or so to get started, then I'll make an assumption–your family is young. If you're older, (say older than 40) and you can barely scrape together $2,000, then you probably need a different book than this one–perhaps a motivational book, or one on vitamin pills. Whatever, young or old, if that's it, then find the most outrageous, crazy, wild, risky plan you can find and go for the gusto. What do you have to lose? Surely you can get back (earn, et cetera) $2,000 to $5,000. In Arizona, they teach you that if you have water (bottle, canteen, et cetera) and you get stranded in the desert – drink it all–now! Apparently our bodies store and ration liquids better than our minds.

If you have $100,000, then take $95,000 and buy safe, secure, blue chip, "hold for the long term" stocks. Be extra safe. Now take $2,000 to $5,000 and go to town. Treat the stock market like a business. Be aggressive.

Read the following interview and see what I mean. The last time I talked to this man, his $20,000 was over $900,000 and that's three to four months after attending my Wall Street Workshop™. He's on target to make over $1,000,000 in one year, from his $20,000.

MYKE L. INTERVIEW

Amy: Why don't you start off by telling me how you heard about Wade.

Myke: The first time I heard about Wade's system was over the radio on a commercial a couple of years ago. I heard it a few times, and got to thinking about how you always hear people say, "Oh, I made money in the Stock market," and the old thought of "buy and hold, buy and hold." I thought the only people who could make money with that strategy are those who bought Microsoft in 1986. It was at $14 or so, and it's split so many times. Wade was talking about 11 different strategies, and I though I wanted to look into this. So I went to a three hour Financial Clinic. It was a good experience, because I really was a total novice and I wanted to learn the language. I learned what a covered call was, about call options, put options, et cetera. And I'll tell you, options scared me when I first heard about it. They painted it real nice for covered calls, so when I got home I got on my spreadsheet and I said,

"Okay, what can I put into it, as a start?" I was very conservative, I put in a little less in my estimate. I started with $5,000 on my estimate at 15%, or 7^1/2% on margin to 15%. I assumed that it would never be called out; it is strictly getting the premium from the covered calls. In three years, starting with $5,000, using $10,000 margin in the beginning, I ended up with about a million dollars. I thought wow, this is kind of cool. I went a little further to five years; it was a couple billion dollars. I then decided that I just going to go out even farther because spreadsheets are easy. I think I'll go out 12 years. It was like a trillion dollars. That'll never happen of course. Anyway, it was fun to look and see what the projections where. They were only projections, but that got me excited by looking at what could be there without having to sell soap with a multi-level marketing company. I didn't have to alienate my friends. It was something I could just do all on the phone or over the Internet and place my order. I do my own investigating and research. I first heard about it over the radio and I thought to myself, "I think I can do that."

Amy: With all the knowledge that you have gained, and all the cash flow that you now know how to make from watching the Wall Street Workshop™ Videos, how do you think that is going to benefit you in your future life, and make you more wise toward your money?

Myke: Yes! Well, ask any of my friends and they will tell that I was extremely tight with my money. When I first got married, earning minimum wage, and barely making ends meet, if I spent a quarter on a candy bar, boom, I wrote it down. I needed to budget where everything went. Since then of course, I've gotten better jobs and all. I have been able to increase my cash flow, increase the money in the bank, and we were able to buy a new place over in Idaho. 56 acres with a 7 bedroom, 4^1/2 bath log house. It's beautiful. We bought it premature in the sense that I'm not retired yet. But it was one of those great deals where if you don't buy it now you're gonna miss it. So, we bring our friends up *on extended weekends, and the whole point was we want them to use it. We can't use it all the time, and we want our friends and family to use it. Having increased my income because of a contract that I'm working on right now, I'm not able to retire. My wife wants to retire and we'll be doing it in about four months. We have four children at home, all ten or younger. We plan on spending more time with them. I'm fairly religious and I don't think God intends the righteous to be poor. He would rather have them have the money. Now, others can too, of course. Because more of them are willing to give to charities, to disburse more, which I have thankfully done. I work with the Boy Scouts of America. I have been doing it for about 15 years. I'm able to purchase some equipment for them, pay for some boys to go to camp that wouldn't be able to otherwise, so that they can enjoy and learn from scouting the same I was able to do as a youth. It changes a person. I started off saying that I was very tight with my money. I'm not as tight now and I feel better about it. But the main thing is I'll be able to spend more time with my family and friends, and to help my friends out. I have a friend now that is changing jobs. He may be without a job for a month or two and I'm going to tell him if he needs help, don't be afraid to ask, because we are in a position to do that. Anybody can do this if they do the research and have the discipline to follow the strategies. Now, I've taken the strategies, looked at individual stocks that I like, and have fine-tuned the strategies to those stocks. Wade and his group have done the research. I am so thankful for Wade Cook because, again, growing up they never taught me this in high school or college. You think, oh buy and hold, and hold it for the rest of your life. That was the mentality of our parents. But nowadays, I think the volatility of the market is due to the younger generation that's putting money into it. Why is it inflated like it is now? Because they know or they sense that Social Security is not going to be there when they retire so they need to find another avenue. We are also the generation that needs a pager, a cell phone, drive-through meals, drive-through laundromat, drive-through* dentistry…I mean everything. And, because of that, they love playing the rolls, the ranges of stocks, and options. Yeah…it goes up…oh, I'm comfortable with this profit, and I will get out. It goes back down…now I think it's a good bottom…boom. They're causing the volatility, and Wade teaches the way to capitalize on that. That's all. He's not teaching anything that Warren Buffett doesn't know, or that any of those other stock traders do. He's just teaching. He's teaching in layman's terms, so any of us simple folk can understand it. And that's what's great about it, because I liken myself to him a little bit. First off, I find myself teaching seminars almost every lunch to people around work. They see that I'm so excited, and because of that, I do what Wade does. Getting back to it, they ask me, "Well, why would Wade do this? Why would anybody, who's made so much money want to tell others?" But, it's just like me. When I get excited about something–I find a sale at a department store–I'll go and tell my friends if I think it's something that they might like. I'm excited about [the stock market] because it is fun; it is almost the adrenaline of the deal. That's why salesmen are so pumped a lot of times. But with [the stock market] you don't have to sell anything, and you don't have to sell anybody. I think I am sort of like Wade in that way. I think more than anything he radiates excitement. When you get involved with his strategies, it is contagious.

Amy: Yea, when Wade speaks he really grabs the attention of everyone; his enthusiasm really is contagious. Tell me, what do you look for in the future as far as your own personal trading?

Myke: Right now I'm doing options. Buying and selling call options, I've done some selling of puts, which I really like. I like selling puts, the last week and a half of an option month with stocks that are going up. There's a great tape that I listen to, 2.3 million. It's an audiotape about the Doctor who made $2.3 million in one year. Yea, I listen to it. I learned a lot about selling puts. I didn't understand puts in the beginning. I listened to the tape, and it became very clear how safe that was. I work a lot *over news that comes out. I'm a computer programmer analyst, so I feel comfortable working with the computer stocks, high tech, even the Internet. Yes, they're very volatile, but I like that. I think volatility, like Wade says, can be capitalized on. Yes, it will go down, buy hey, it will go right back up. There's actually a lot of time value premium placed in the option price. And so, I plan on doing that, and like I mentioned, I plan on retiring in about four months. I'll hit about a million; that will be approximately a little over a year that I've been doing options, starting with $36,000. And then that's a million profits. Then what I plan on doing is pulling it all out but $250,000 in my account and work it. I figure if you can't make it on $250,000 starting with $36,000, then you're doing something wrong. I'll take the rest out and pay my taxes. At that point I plan on becoming a Nevada Corporation. That will help to protect it. I'll set up my pension plan, then take the rest of my money and pay off all my bills, pay off the home we're in now, then the 56 acres up in Idaho, and pay off all of our vehicles. The future, though, I see as continually trading. It is so fun. It's not a job, it is a hobby. And it is an exciting hobby. And that's what you have to do: make it your hobby. Anything you do needs to be a hobby.*

Projections look great, and I was so excited when I did my first option. I bought Microsoft right after their 2:1 split announcement, and 8 days later I sold it. I invested $22,000 and made a profit of $18,000, or about 80%, in 8 days. It was about a 3,600% annual return.

I use W.I.N.™ and I use IQ Pager™. With IQ Pager™ I've made probably made at least 10 fold this year alone off of it. One example was Chrysler. When Chrysler came out on IQ Pager™ one morning and it said that Chrysler was in talks with Daimler-Benz Mercedes to potentially be bought out. I thought, "Well, I'll buy 1,000 options shares, or 10 contracts. It was at $4³/4. I thought it will take a month or two before they do it. Next day BOOM, they announced they were going to merge. The option went from

$4³/₄ up to $8¹/₄. I sold that day and earned about 80 or 85% profit. Annualized that was 14,000 plus percent profit. Some people say do not look at your annualized return, or you can't do that. But hey, banks do it; I do it only for fun, just to see what it would be.

I'll tell you, I listen to talk radio, and a lot of it is on financial programming. People would call in and they are always talking about mutual funds. Hey, mutual funds are a great portion of your portfolio. It's a great thing; it's good and stable. But people would call up and say, "Well gee. I've got a mutual fund that earned me 14% last year. I'm looking to moving to a 16% mutual fund, but I'll have to pay a penalty…etc." That's 14% per year. I'd kind of shake my head and say, "You know, if they only knew about or took the step to learn some of these strategies, they could earn so much more." For example, in 10 months this year alone—the time I've done options—I've done 1300% profit.

Amy: And they're doing 14%?

Myke: And they're doing 14% a year with mutual funds, and the comparison is 1300% a year. Now not everybody's going to do that, but I will say that during that 10 months we had our 1998 bear market. In fact, I started with $36,000 invested in February of that year. By August 26ᵗʰ I had $112,000 profit, so it quadrupled. Five days later, because of the bear market, I was down to only 36% profit. So, I dropped that much. Now, I wasn't that concerned because you don't lose money until you sell. If you remember that, you're not going to panic and get stressed out as much. But let's say that was on August 31ˢᵗ. On December 29, 1998, I was up to $470,000. So basically starting with $36,000, in three and a half months I was up to $470,000 profit. Not everybody's going to do that, but yes, we have our little bear corrections. This one was, I believe, 4 to 6 weeks. A lot of my portfolio was flat or going down. But right afterwards, boom! It shot back up. A lot of people may have gotten out and said, "Hey, I can't handle this." But mine shot up; I happened to pick some by searching them out; yes, they were high tech–the Internet went crazy. But hey, anybody could've done it and a lot of people did. So, I guess for me it was just a matter of learning the strategies, gathering as much information as I could, and going out and testing it.

Amy: Did you have any trading background before you knew about Wade?

Myke: I had no trading experience before I met Wade Cook. Like I said, all I knew was the age-old method of buy and hold. I didn't own any stock. The only bonds I held were savings bonds. I had a 401(k) that I'd keep in the stock fund and it was about 30% a year with matching. That was fantastic until I started figuring Wade's stuff out. And again, the first thing I investigated was covered calls. That was 15% potentially a month. Wow, a month! In two months I could meet what I did in my company's 401K plan. It's a matter of being proactive. It's also a matter of getting excited and making it a hobby. When I say making it a hobby, I don't mean it's a chore. If you're not really into it, you're not going to succeed, and not because you're not talented. Oh, you could succeed, don't get me wrong, but it's fun to have that burning desire to go out and do it. And you know it's funny, I need to say this. I had friends of mine look at me and say, "You know, you're obsessed with making money. Just obsessed with it because you're always talking about it." And you know it's funny, it's usually the ones that aren't willing to do it.

And my rebuttal to them is, "Really? And how many hours do you spend at work? How many hours do you spend commuting?"

"Well, about 2 hours–an hour each way."

"So, 10 hours a day. I spend about 30 minutes a day. When I retire I'll still spend 30 minutes a day. Am I obsessed, or are you?"

Amy: So you have been trading for a little over a year?

Myke: Correct.

Amy: If you don't mind, what did you start out with?

Myke: The amount?

Amy: Yes.

Myke: I first started out with $6,000; it was actually our tax returns. And I started doing covered calls with that. The first covered call I did was Office Depot. They were in talks with Staples to be bought out. It was at $18¹/₄. I bought it at $18¹/₄, and sold the $20 option for the next month out for $2. Now, since I bought it on margin, I only paid half. I got $1,000 before commissions. But what's interesting is after that, I turned the $1,000 and bought 100 more shares and sold one more contract at a little higher premium and made a little more in percentage. The first one I did about 21%, the second one I did about 23%. But the second 23% was a profit on profit. And of that first thousand, five hundred of it, technically, was from someone else–by broker– through the margin account.

And it's interesting; I called in on a financial show on the radio because they were asking for people who'd made money through Wade Cook, somebody who actually made money. That's why I called in. He asked me what I did and I told him about my Office Depot trade. So he said, "Oh, so you earned about 10.5%."

I said, "No, I earned 21%."

"Oh, you did margin; oh that's risky."

So I said, "Really? Why is that?"

"Well, because you're borrowing someone else's money."

And I said "Well, you know, the way it was explained to me by my broker is that basically if you buy a $10 stock, it has to drop all the way to about $3 or $4 before you get a margin call. If it drops that much, you didn't pick very well."

And so I mentioned to this host on the radio that out of the $1,000 in the first month, basically $500 of it was from their money that I borrowed. And that first month I paid them 8¼% interest, or $22 for the money I borrowed. So if you look at it, if I hand you $22, are you going to hand me $500? That's a heck of a deal. But that's the way it is and that's why margin really is not that scary once you understand that principle.

Amy: Are you doing more covered calls now?

Myke: Covered calls? No, I am using straight options: call options and some selling of put options. Covered calls I do in my IRA account because it's so safe that the IRS lets you do that in an IRA.

Amy: That's cool.

Myke: I haven't been working that account as much because I can't get at it until I'm 59, so why work it?

Amy: What do you think about the quality of the Wall Street Workshop™ Videos that you purchased?

Myke: The quality was great. I thought it was very good and extremely professional. I've seen other videos that you rent at the video store that aren't as good, and these are supposed to be these million dollar movies; they're B movies is what they are. But I was very impressed with the Wall Street Videos. I thought that Wade covered it great. One thing that I really like about Wade is the way he talks. I learned a lot from it; they are well organized and the videos were fantastic. The audiotapes are really also good because you're actually not hearing the lectures that you're used to in college where they put you to sleep. And it's not just Wade, it's other instructors. There's excitement in there because they do the deals. They not only do the deals; they make money off the *deals. Sometimes they use their own accounts and so you see that on the video, you hear it on the audiotapes, plus they're talking with the brokers right there. Granted, they may be a year or two old, but so what! Don't fall into the same concern that I had when I first got started, that I needed to jump in now because I heard there was going to be a stock split by Microsoft; if I miss this one, I will never make any money. I have played Microsoft five times, I've played Dell four times, I've played Amazon.com four times. Yahoo a number of times, Chrysler, and Boeing. I've played some smaller ones too. A lot of the smaller ones I got off the IQ Pager. But getting back to the videos, they're great. It is extremely professional, and like I said, when Wade teaches he's just bubbling with excitement.*

Amy: It's contagious.

Myke: It really is. What's really funny is that years ago you used to hear about real estate. I know Wade does real estate seminars. I never went to those. I thought about it, but I always thought, "Wait a minute, why are these guys teaching it, because there is limited supply of good deals in real estate." There is not a limited supply necessarily in stocks, but there is in real estate. So in the back of my mind I was wondering, "Now hey, would these guys be out on the circuit teaching these? Has it dried up? Is that how they're making their money now, doing this?" But with Wade, whether it's on W.I.N.™ or over at the Wall Street Workshops™ with other instructors, they are actually doing the trades. Good or bad, gains or losses, you are looking over their shoulder when it comes to W.I.N.™. Every trading day, they've got Wall Street Workshops™ going on out there and they submit their trades. Then Wade will come in and say, "Well gee, today on the way to basketball I went ahead and did these trades here. I did a bull put spread, I did covered calls here, I did a call there, I did an option there," and you're actually seeing it. Then maybe a couple of weeks later, "Well, I made money on these, I didn't make money on those, they just weren't doing good. The strategy was good, but the stock itself didn't pan out. Maybe bad news came out or something, so I sold." But he's willing to tell you. I wonder about a lot of others because, hey, it's a guy thing okay? Men are very proud and they don't like to show weakness. That's just the way it is, I'm sorry. And yet, it's funny because I show the people at work a spreadsheet of my trades and there are a lot of them where I lost. They weren't the big money losses, but hey, I show 'em. Like Wade says in his books, "Keep a record of why you bought and why you sold because it is not a strategy unless it can be repeated." If you keep a record of why you did such and such, maybe you lost money on it, okay, why? Say I'm interested in that stock again, but why did I sell? Did I sell early? Yes, I did. I bought because there was a dip and earnings were expected to come out strong. I sold two days before because the history says that it goes down right when their positive earnings come out. At the same time I bought a put option because it goes down historically. Keep a record of that so you can go back, plus you can hand it to your friends. I always have my friends say, "Tell you what. Let me give you the money. You do the trades for me and I'll give you 10%."

I look at them and say, "No, I'll give you 10%, but I won't do it for you, but I'll teach you how to do it." And it's fun. My mom was a schoolteacher and my brother is a teacher. I didn't go into teaching because the money wasn't there, and I didn't know if I'd have the patience with kids. I do teach the Boy Scouts. I love teaching people, those that want to learn. And it's just fun; it really is fun.

Amy: Is there anything else you want to say that you haven't already?

Myke: I think I've covered a lot. You can always call me back if you have any questions or if someone listens to it and then wants to get a little more information on something. You can do that for them.

Okay, let's say he only makes $250,000 on the initial $5,000. Let's say that's you. You are two days of training away from having the skills to do this. If it is you, and you are into safety, remember, you have your $95,000 worth of good, solid investments to make you feel good at night and when you get your portfolio statement. Hopefully, the dividends and growth of the stocks will give you 10% plus per year. That could be $10,000 (of which only a small portion is cash). You've got the best of both worlds; aggressive cash flow and stability.

ADD TO YOUR POSITIONS

Now, let's move on. Take $100,000 or even $200,000 and buy more blue chips. Take the other $50,000 (or more) and keep it generating cash flow. You see, that's the point I've been making at my seminars and in my writings. Use the formulas for income generation to build up your cash flow, so you can accelerate the purchase of stocks in great blue chip companies or to pay the bills.

On the opposite page is a list of my cash flow strategies.

Most of these strategies are to be used for cash flow. They put the emphasis on selling–getting out. You only purchase them to resell them at a profit. They deal with two-week and one-month 15 to 55% returns. They spin off cash. Real money. "Send me a check and let's go shopping" type of money!

THE REST OF THE GUYS

1. *Long-term hold:*
   - *Blue Chip Stocks*
   - *Bargain Stocks*
   - *Mutual Funds, REITS, et cetera*

THE WADE COOK WAY

1. *Long-term hold:*
   - *Blue Chip Stocks*
   - *Bargain Stocks*
   - *Mutual Funds, REITS, et cetera.*
2. *Rolling Stocks: Buy and sell on repeated and predictable patterns (highs and lows).*
3. *Options: Proxy investing—low cost, limited risk options for safety investing.*
4. *Writing Covered Calls: Generate income monthly on stocks you own or buy.*
5. *Stock Splits: (and other news) There are five strategies to enter and exit stocks or options doing splits.*
6. *Sell Puts: Generate income—get paid now.*
7. *Bull Put Spreads: Generate income, limit risk, lessen margin.*
8. *Bull Call Spreads: Writing covered calls by covering with options.*
9. *Bargain Hunting: Bottom fishing for long-term hold or quick pops.*
10. *Spin-offs: Capture the stock—buy options on stock.*
11. *IPOs: If not at first, wait, get in and out. Use 25 day IPO rule.*
12. *Turnarounds: Catch the wave up and do stocks or proxy investing.*
13. *Slams and Peaks: (Really two strategies). Catch the turn one to five day plays. Quick cash.*
14. *Range Riders: (Bonus Strategy) Buy and sell at tops and bottoms all the way up.*

If you choose, you can use some or all of this cash flow to build a wonderful, safe, "proud to own" portfolio. But one which accumulates quickly because you're able to add to it repeatedly, month after month, with the profits from the smaller cash flow part of your system.

The following shows the major difference between Stock Market Institute of Learning, Inc.™ and all the other financial professionals.

STOCKBROKERS	STOCK MARKET INSTITUTE OF LEARNING™
1. They receive commissions for selling investments, regardless of returns to client.	1. We sell no investments. We teach strategies for wise decision making and the generation of cash flow. We get nothing out of what our students make.
2. They advise clients on specific investments.	2. We explain formulas, methods, and techniques to work the market. Stocks are mentioned as working examples. No specific advice is given.
3. Many financial professionals get paid a percentage of the assets they manage, whether assets increase or decrease.	3. We teach. The students learn and earn. They work the formulas, after paper or Simutrading™, and keep all the profits. We help investors choose better stockbrokers and how to work better with them.
4. They sometimes get investors involved in risky investments.	4. We show students how to avoid and minimize risk with a dedication to knowledge and specific tools like low-cost options, spreads, puts on increased values and writing covered calls.
5. They preach "asset allocation" placing portions of investor's money in harm's way.	5. We teach how to use a diversity of formulas for cash flow, tax write-offs, and growth. We help students learn to find certain stocks/options that fit the formulas.
6. They constantly sell investors the new "investment du jour."	6. We teach and show investors how to work the formulas, spread out risk, avoid losses and not get caught up in erratic and fad investments.

7. *Some move money in and out to generate commissions.*	7. *We are an unbiased educational source. We get nothing out of what our students do. We only talk about a stock or option if it fits one of our cash flow or wealth building formulas.*
8. *Most do not show their trading results, they surely do not publicize their personal trades.*	8. *We tell all, show all. All trades are listed on our award winning Internet site at wadecook.com.* Current subscribers tap into this informative tutorial service. Anyone can scroll back and see all trades (the when, where, how to, and why to).*
9. *Many are single-minded. They have their products for sale. They are concerned about their commissions with little regard*	9. *We teach, show and expound on five holistic financial topics: We teach how to make money (actual cash flow) in business, in the stock market and in real estate. We show how to reduce exposure to liability and risk through the use of different entities. We show business people how to reduce their tax liability. We show people how to prepare for a great retirement. We show people how to bequeath all posessions in a "TLC" way.*

*Chosen by readers of Securities Traders Handbook as the web site with the most new investment ideas.

THE WADE COOK WAY

The Wade Cook way is simple–simple rules to follow. It is methods or formulas. It is the formatting of a process. It is having a plan. You, for example, do not get greedy on any one deal. We're not trying to buy one stock by buying an apartment complex and having it grow into millions of dollars. We're buying a stock at $92, hoping that it goes to $104, and then we're going to get out. You don't get greedy.

The next part of the Wade Cook way is to think big. Think cash flow rich, but in small, bite size pieces. Doable, functional, reliable if you will, predictable, bite size pieces.

A crucial element in the Wade Cook way is to always know your exit before you ever go in the entrance. I know a lot of you have heard this for years now. Know your exit. Don't get involved in a strategy unless you know exactly where you're going to get uninvolved. See, you can't do that with a traditional business. You can't start up a business, and then say, "I'm going to own this business for a year and a half and then sell it at 'X'". Right? You can try that, but when you go to sell it you have to find a buyer, list it, and then it could take months to sell. The stock market, I submit to you, makes an incredible, part-time business. And it could become full-time.

You've heard me say, "treat the stock market like a business". Buy low, sell high. Buy wholesale, sell retail. How about if I changed it and said, "treat the stock market like a job." I wanted to fight that for awhile. "Don't treat the stock market like a job", I said. But you know what, the more I think about it, the more I realize that you should treat it like a job. Make it develop into a career. Get good at it. Get to be an expert at an angle to it.

All right, so, what is the Wade Cook way, besides those three things I just mentioned? You know, bite-size pieces, knowing your exit, and treating it like a business.

Part of my way is to use low-cost, limited-risk, leverage type trading. For example: options. I'll give you a simple example. You really like Microsoft. Microsoft is sitting around $94. My goodness, to buy a thousand shares of Microsoft would cost $94,000. Even if your broker let's you do it on margin, which means that they'll put up half the money, it's still $47,000, and you now *own* a thousand shares of Microsoft. Is there a way to get the benefits of Microsoft going up in value without risking so much capital? If you really think it's going to go to $102 or $108, then call your stockbroker and ask, "What does it cost to buy an *option* to buy Microsoft stock?" He may say to you, "Well, it would depend on the strike price."

Now the strike prices in that range are in $5 increments, so you could talk about an $85, $90, $95 or $100 strike price. Let's say that you think Microsoft is going up in a month or two and you get the $95 call. That gives you the right–you don't have any obligation–to buy the stock at $95. The stock is currently at $94. Just stop right here and think this through! Your broker tells you the price of the $95 call is $6. To control one hundred shares the cost would be $600. To control that *same thousand* shares of stock would be $6,000, *not* $94,000, *not* $47,000 if you were to do it on margin. For $6,000 you have locked down the right to buy Microsoft at $95 for the next month or two. Now, if that stock goes up to $98, my goodness, $94,000 to $98,000, would be a $4,000 profit if you owned the stock and sold it. But if you own that $6,000 option, what if the option only went up one or two dollars? Your $6,000 is now $8,000. If you were to sell, you would have $8,000 cash back into your account in one day. You have a $2,000 profit, minus the commissions.

All right, where's the better return? Well, the better return is in owning the stock. You entered the trade with $94,000 cash, and now you have $98,000. You would have made a $4,000 profit. But, what's the better *rate* of return? Making a $2,000 profit on your investment of $6,000, or $4,000 on the move from $94,000 to $98,000? I think you start to get the point. You can, with a small amount of leverage, called stock options, increase your rate of return substantially.

Then you ask, "What about the downside, what about the risk? What if Microsoft tanks? What if it goes down?" All right, let's go there for a minute. What if it does go down? What if Microsoft, as soon as you bought it, has all this news coming out? You think it's the hot stock, you think it's going up, and instead of going from $94 right up to $98, it goes from $94 down to $85. What do you do now? Well, again, if you follow the Wade Cook way and know your exit before you go into the entrance, you would have had stop losses in place. So, your $6,000 cash that you had invested, as soon as it gets down to $4,000 or $3,000, you're out with a $3,000 loss. That's all you can lose.

Our stockbrokers, bless their hearts, will let us buy that stock, and they'll sit there and bad-mouth options if they don't understand them. As soon as they understand them, they quit bad-mouthing them, like almost anything else. "If you're not up on it, you're down on it." If they don't get it, they bad-mouth it.

So your $6,000 goes down to $3,000, or even down to zero! Your risk is that you may lose your whole $6,000. However, with options you get all the upside potential. My goodness, if Microsoft goes to $110 or $120, your $6,000 could turn into $18,000 or $24,000. You could get a triple, or a quadruple on your money! What's your down-side risk? $6,000. You tell me which risk is greater. If Microsoft tanks, $94,000 down to $85,000, you lose $9,000 if you own the stock! If you own the option, you lose your $6,000. And if you knew your exit, you got out before it dropped all the way down to zero. Do you see the point? Where do you have limited downside risk, but unlimited upside potential? That is what stock options provide for you. Are they for everyone? Nope. You really need to understand them. You need to understand the time-sensitive nature of options. That's one thing we really stress at our two-day, experiential learning formatted Wall Street Workshop™. This process becomes a formula and a profitable "cash flow" formula, at that.

Now once we understand what an option is, then what we really need to know is how to play it and where to go with it. It's just like if you're learning how to play the piano. I can teach you what the notes are. I can teach you where middle C is. I can teach you that by playing C, E, and G, you get a C chord. I can teach you all that. But you aren't playing the piano until you sit down at the keys with music and learn how to play a song. So I guess what I'm trying to say is that our company teaches you *how to play the songs*. Once you know how to play, you can apply the notes, those chords, those runs, to any song. That's what we try to show in the stock market. There are things that you can do to learn how to "trade in" the stock market.

I know a lot of people have heard me talk about our company and what we do. I would like to address an issue right now that I think will shock a lot of you. I don't know why, but the last couple of years, Wade Cook—me personally, and our company in general—has become a lightening rod for a lot of negative criticism. Now, when I hear that, I kind of chuckle and laugh under my breath. I wear the criticism as a badge of honor, because they just don't get it. They just don't understand. I have received criticism by people who have written books. Why do they have to criticize mine? If they have a message, if they have a song to sing, why don't they just sing it? But, apparently they have to bad-mouth me, when they don't even understand what I do. They don't read my books. They just criticize and say, "Wade Cook talks about risky investments." Excuse me? We talk about spreads, and how to control that downside risk. We are here to show people how to safely preserve their asset base, at whatever level, and have that base grow and produce income. That's what our company is about.

Say they take $2,000 into one of the big brokerage firms and say, "I've only got $2,000 and I want it to produce six or seven hundred dollars a month extra income for me." Do you think they're going to do that? No. As a matter of fact, I've seen (I won't name any names) some of these ads on TV where these big, huge brokerage firms have on-line Internet access for your account. This is the age of the individual investor, empowering individual people to make a lot of money and to take control of their own financial destiny.

That's where we are today with the Internet and information readily accessible. They say, "We help investors learn all this stuff." I beg your pardon. I've gone to their site because I have an account there, and I said, "You know, I would sure like to get some information on 'Writing a Covered Call.' I want to use existing stocks for generating income by 'selling options.'" I did not find *one* piece of information about Writing a Covered Call. I wondered if they had information about channeling or Rolling Stocks. This is a strategy where stocks go between two price points: down to a support level, and up to a resistance, and in repeated waves. Up and down, up and down. We can buy and sell, buy and sell, and make a lot of money. There was not *one* piece of information on channeling or Rolling Stocks.

Oh, well, maybe they have information on Stock Split strategies. We have five unique times to get involved, and exit strategies to get uninvolved. So, I go looking for this type of information. *Nothing.*

So, I go looking for information on spreads. My favorite strategy of all strategies is our incredible Bull Put Spread. I cannot find one piece of information. You know what I did find? I found information about XYZ Company, or I find information about this mutual fund. What is their job? They're a stock brokerage outfit. How do they make money? How do they pay their bills? By selling you another investment. Whether that investment makes money or not, they sell investments. We don't sell investments. We teach formulas, and strategies for continued success.

So when I see all these people trying to take the "high road," I'm puzzled. We are the *only* high road. We don't get anything out of what our customers do. We teach formulas. We teach methods. They *learn* them, and then they *earn* from them. That is who we are. And we're just going to keep on doing that. Come hell or high water, we're going to defend the right of small individual investors to continue to make money, so they can quit their jobs! So two parents don't both have to work!

Now, our methods provide a unique opportunity for you to define who you are. When you're trying to decide, "What type of trader am I? What type of investor am I? Should I be buying and holding? Should I be buying stocks for the long run because I'm so busy? I'm making so much money with my career, heavens I just need to park my money in a bunch of mutual funds." Or, are you saying, "I need to buy and sell, buy and sell, buy and sell several times a month and make $1,000 there, $1,500 here, and $800 there. I need to start making some money." You need to decide who you are.

2

TREAT IT AS A BUSINESS

C an you get rich working for someone else? Probably not, unless you make excess income and then get that extra income producing great returns.

Can you get rich owning your own business? Yes, but most businesses fail. Even if the business does not fail, most take up too much of the owner's (manager's) time working on things which do not make him or her rich.

Is the American Dream still alive and well?

It truly is.

One secret of wealth accumulation has been that little extra something put aside and left to compound. Is the time right for you to "get rich?" After all, someone becomes a millionaire every 37 minutes. When is it going to be your turn? What superior knowledge do you have? What risks are you willing to take? What time can you donate to making a great financial life? This chapter is about getting wealthy–filthy rich if you want, with more income than you can possibly spend. I have thought long and hard about what I could write, what I could do to help you become a "cash flow millionaire." I want you to read every word of this. Do not skip anything. I will build a case for you and show you in many ways that you can build up $12,000 to $35,000 per month cash flow—and do it in the next year. I will show you how to do it without vitamin pills, or any other multilevel concern. I will show you how to do it by first eliminating risk—or at least making risk so negligible as to make it a non-item.

You can use bear market strategies in the midst of a bull market, and you can get started with $500 if that is all you have. It is doable. I have made tens of thousands of dollars a day—if you attend a stock market training session we will show you how you can build up your level of income. And you do not have to go through nine years of costly trial and error like I did. You will not have to be at the mercy of unscrupulous and unintelligent stockbrokers, as I have been. You can cut to the chase, start making huge returns in days, and keep all your profits.

You might be asking yourself, "How can Wade possibly be talking about the stock market? Especially when funds managers claim bragging rights with 12% returns?" Can investing really produce 18 to 42% monthly returns—month in and month out? Probably not investing, buy by trading you definitely can. And by the way, I'm not talking about day trading as defined by S.O.E.S. trading. I think S.O.E.S. trading is inappropriate for almost all investors and traders. And what kind of returns are these? I will answer all of those questions, but for now allow me to start with the last question. The kind of returns I am speaking of are actual cash—either hitting your account or mailed to your home or business. It is not growth, not tax savings, but money you can use.

For awhile—at least in the beginning—I suggest you use this extra money for portfolio enhancement, either building more cash flow by doing more of what you did to make this money, or buying some "hold" investments; or applying it to other formulas. Later, with a small amount of money, delve into riskier but incredibly profitable strategies to really make a big "bang" on your bottom line. Regardless of your choice, your return is in cash, not some poor substitute. I have always contended that *we*—you and I and all my other students—can make more together than we ever can alone. It is true. I will lead the way. I will try and test new ideas, formulas, strategies, processes—you come along, buy my books, attend my ongoing classes, and then make cash flow, spending your profits the way you like.

Each person who attends my seminars does so for his own personal reasons. Some are just getting started and need to learn the basics, others are in business or want to be, and need help "growing" their business. Others are making good money but paying a high price in terms of stress, time away from their families, et cetera. Others have tax problems, and a host of others are in various stages and want to learn how to keep and protect what they have as well as pass on what they have "scraped" together throughout their lives. And while they come for various reasons, they all have one thing in common–they know there is a better way. A more excellent way, if you will. What is the saying, "Winners just find a better way to get there?"

Now that I have asked all these questions, who is this person asking these questions? Let me introduce myself briefly. I realize you may not know anything about me, my background, or to what extent it will help you make more money. So I will be brief, but you need to walk in my shoes for a moment. I cannot help you in the present unless you know what got me here, what drives me, my fears and passions.

History

When I was young, my goals were not lofty. I didn't want to be President of the United States or conquer the world. My dream was to become a college professor. To educate myself to reach my dream, I needed income. I could not get any money from my parents, and because we were a middle class family, it was hard to get college grants and loans.

To generate income, I started up an insurance agency. I figured that if I wrote enough policies, I could have continual income from premiums–at least enough to support me through college. But as hard as I worked to get policies on the books, it was still hard to get paid. I was successful, but it just wasn't enough.

So I made two moves that changed my life permanently. First, inspired by the book *How I Took a Thousand Dollars and Made Five Million Investing in Real Estate* by William Nickerson, I turned to real estate. I borrowed money to buy my first couple of properties.

Second, simply out of the need to buy groceries for my family, I latched onto a job driving a taxicab. Have you ever had one of those experiences that afterwards continues to change just about everything else you do? Driving a taxi was just such an experience for me.

In order for you to understand what this is all about, you need to come back with me to my first day driving a cab. The company I started driving for, Yellow Cab Company in Tacoma, Washington, had a mandatory rule that entailed spending a day training with a cab driver/ trainer named Bill Marsh.

After being out with Bill for about 45 minutes (30 minutes at Denny's getting him a cup of coffee) I realized that I could handle this cab driving business on my own. As I watched what he did, it dawned on me that to be a successful cab driver you only had to do one thing.

I asked Bill if he would take me back to the lobby to get my own taxi. He said I had to spend the whole "mandatory" day with him. "Look," I said, "could you please just take me back?"

Back at the cab company I talked to the owner/partner. "Mrs. Potter?" I said, "My name is Wade Cook. I'm a brand new cab driver. You don't know me, but is there any way I can just take a taxi out for the day?"

She replied, "Oh no, no. You have to spend the day with Bill Marsh."

I persisted. I explained to her that I knew Tacoma really well and told her that if she didn't like what I did by five or six o'clock that afternoon, she would never see me again. She listened and ended up giving me a little beat-up Dodge Dart for the day.

I took it out that first day and made $110–that was my net. The second day I came back with about $90 profits and the third day about $140. I was off and running. I began making between $3,200 and $3,800 a month. I needed about $1,200 a month to live on. I was able to take the rest, holding some out for taxes, and apply it to buying and fixing up houses. With this money, I purchased nine rental houses my first year. The rest of my real estate story is told in the books *Real Estate Money Machine, How To Pick Up Foreclosures, Real Estate for Real People,* and *101 Ways to Buy Real Estate Without Cash.*

My point here is the lesson I learned in driving a taxi–to me the most significant and powerful financial lesson I have ever learned in my life. In fact, since then I've hobnobbed with some of the greatest financial minds in the country (doing radio, TV talk shows and seminars in 43 different states), and nothing I've learned from any of those men and women is more powerful than what I learned my first day driving a cab. The lesson is simply this–*money is made in the meter drop.*

What does "the meter drop" mean? Every time you get into a taxi, the driver pushes the meter down (nowadays it's a computerized button), and it costs you $1.50 to $2. Whether it is a $5 run or a $50 run, you still pay $1.50 every time you get in the cab.

Many cab drivers only take big runs. In Tacoma they positioned themselves in town to get the run to Sea-Tac Airport, a $30 to $35 fare. At the same time, I was beating the cab to death by going for all the small runs. I would take the $3, $6 and $8 runs. At the end of some busy days I would have up to 40, 50, or 60 runs. You see the difference? I was killing them. Now, don't get me wrong, I've had my share of big runs too. Sometimes a little $6 run would turn into a $15 run because the person my passenger was going to visit wasn't home. However, it was those extra meter drops really added up to a lot of cash.

REPETITIVE CASH FLOW

This made it clear to me that the bottom line to wealth is duplication and repetition. A hamburger in Tampa Bay must taste just like a hamburger in San Francisco Bay, and McDonalds took advantage of this, not by selling one gigantic hamburger, but by selling billions of little ones–and French fries. Repetition made the McDonalds fortune.

About nine months after I started driving, Mrs. Potter called us all in for a meeting between shifts. While we were waiting for her to come in, all the cab drivers were bragging about how much money they were making. Bill Marsh sat there and said he had made more money in one month than anybody there. I casually asked him how much he made. With a note of triumph, he said, "One month I made $900." All the cab drivers started oohing over him, thinking that $900 was a lot of money.

Now remember, my lowest month was over $3,200. But I said with a smile, "Boy, that is a lot of money, Bill." No way was I going to mention to these guys how much I was making. They could see the rental properties I was buying and draw their own conclusions, but to this day, they still don't know.

On to real estate. At first, I did not follow the lesson I learned as a cab driver. I went out and started the old buy-and-wait game. I waited for inflation, waited for Washington D.C. tax write offs, and waited for other things I had no control over. After a year of playing the buy-and-wait game–the rental game–I had to sell one of my properties. I desperately needed money. I sold the property, received some cash for the down payment and carried back a mortgage. The key, however, is that I didn't get all cash up front. I sold the property under what you would call "owner financing."

I sat in my taxi staring at the check I received from the down payment, and realized something. I had purchased this little property with $1,200 down. When I sold it, even after closing costs, I still ended up with $2,200–$1,000 more than I put into this property in the beginning. And, I would receive net monthly payments of $125 for 28 years.

I just stared at the check. I had stumbled across a whole new way of investing. I thought, why am I playing this buy-and-wait game? Why am I turning my life over to renters? Why wait for tax write offs out of Washington D.C., hoping some benevolent congressman gets a depreciation bill passed through Congress? Why am I doing things I have no control over? Why don't I just go out and buy properties to sell? *Why not do the meter drop with my properties?*

I figured that I could sell a couple more rentals right away and then target properties I could buy and fix up a little bit, then turn around and sell on this "money machine."

Back then, I did not call it the "Money Machine." I called this "turning properties" or "flipping properties." Nevertheless, I realized that I had to treat real estate like the "meter drop." Instead of getting in and waiting, why not just buy for the sole purpose of reselling? This way I could build up a huge base of deeds of trust and mortgages and have monthly checks coming in. In the end it was these monthly checks that allowed me, and will allow you, to live the way we want.

At that time I had a lot of rental properties, but they were only making a little bit of money. If one renter didn't pay one month, it ruined the profits for the whole month. I was constantly putting more money into taking care of these properties. Any of you who have had rental properties realize that no matter what kind of money you have lying around in the bank, any rental property will "eat it up" and take it away from you. The giant "sucking sound" is real.

The rental game is just not what it is cracked up to be. However, the "Money Machine" is a fabulous way to make money by literally forcing the issue–rapidly accumulating wealth. I did this over the next year. I went out specifically looking for properties I could buy and sell quickly. Again, it was the meter drop. Get the passenger in, get the passenger out, and get on to the next trip. After doing many of these properties, I was able to quit and retire at the age of 29.

ON TO THE STOCK MARKET

Faced with time and financial freedom, I ended up writing a book. I never did go back to college to get my teaching degree, but I did end up with a book in the bookstores. Since that time, I have written several more. I entered the lecture circuit and started traveling the country. My semi-retired state was really becoming a fun career. This also gave me the opportunity to make more money.

I knew I didn't want to put the excess money into savings accounts. I did buy a lot of second mortgages, which kept my cash flow ever increasing. In addition, $5,000 here and $10,000 there went into stock market investments.

I opened up a brokerage account and bought mutual funds, one of which had gone up in value 14% each of the previous three years. As soon as I bought it, it went down 2%. Quite a few stocks went up in value, but most of them floundered around and many went down. I figured the stock market was not for me, because I was going to have to learn a whole new set of rules and vocabulary to be successful at it. Meanwhile, I was still involved with real estate and teaching seminars.

Then I got a call from a friend who at that time was a stockbroker. He wanted to take me to lunch and explain what he was doing with many of his clients.

At lunch that day, I listened to a most fascinating idea, which struck a responsive chord telling me it was right and true, especially at that time. He wanted me to buy 100 shares of Motorola stock. (I don't do this with Motorola any more. The stock started to climb up to $100 a share and has since had two 2:1 splits. The stock went back down to $50 and is now trading at around $140 a share. Maybe it will roll again, but I am just not sure.)

I bought 100 shares of Motorola at $50 a share for $5,000 plus $80 in commissions. The stockbroker asked me to put the stock up for sale at $60. Those of you who are familiar with the stock market and have brokerage accounts realize that you can put an order in to sell and take off for Hawaii. If, and when, the stock hits $60 a share, the sale will be triggered automatically by computer.

I put in the order to sell at $60 a share. About six weeks later, the stock hit $60 and the computer sold it. I had $6,000 in my account, minus another $90 in commissions. I made about $830 profit on this transaction. Then the stockbroker said to put in an order to buy the stock again at $50 a share. I put in an order for 108 shares at $50. About five weeks later the stock rolled backed down to $50 and the computer triggered a buy. Now I was the owner of 108 shares of Motorola at $50 a share.

At that time, the stock dropped down to around $48 or $49, and I was getting kind of worried. But it climbed right back up to $60 a share and the computer triggered a sale again. I had the excess profit in my account. The stock rolled from $50 to $60 a share several times and kept climbing up to $61 to $62, so I did miss out on some of the profits, but who cares. The money (cash flow) is in the repetitive rolls. I did this particular stock many times for several years.

This cab driver had found a way to do a meter drop on Wall Street.

I contend that the stock market makes a perfect home-based business and/or a perfect place to develop extra income even if you are working or relying on an existing business. I am convinced that in every respect and aspect it is far superior to most other businesses. I have had a lot of businesses, from one-man shows to a large (in my estimation) 300+ employee corporation. Currently I am CEO and President of Wade Cook Financial Corporation–whose main subsidiary, Stock Market Institute of Learning, Inc., is a powerhouse.

I have taken years to build the business and took it public in May of 1995. I only bring this up because I have employees, payroll taxes, advertising, and every other outlay of cash as well as concerns and considerations associated with running a large business. At times the "busyness" gets in the way of my true loves: family, teaching and working the brokerage accounts. I have tried to blend them together. I do owe an allegiance to my shareholders to be profitable. I have to make public how I work my stock and option deals in the corporate accounts. It is fun, profitable, and is building a tidy fortune for my immediate family (wife and children) and my shareholder family.

I realize that as I make a case for treating the stock market like a business, that I am competing with every "Amway" type company out there. My story is different though, because I am not inviting you to join my "downline." I want you to make a ton of bucks and keep *all* of them. I judge my success as an educator, not by how much I put into people, but how much they get (earn) out of what I teach. The business comparison can go a long way because you are probably familiar with most aspects (whether you are actually experienced or not) of running a business. Indeed, being familiar with what it takes to be successful may have caused you to get into business. We will dispel some falsehoods in a most unusual way. I will approach the comparison of using the stock market as a business by first stating that we are going to take a totally unconventional approach to creating a stock market income portfolio.

If you like mutual funds, or if you are happy with 6 to 10% annual returns, or if you are happy with the boring investments your stockbroker recommends, you probably should not read on. If you want some excitement, then join me as we turn the stock market into a business. I'll take a problem/solution approach:

PROBLEM #1 GETTING STARTED

Most small businesses require substantial up-front costs to get up and going, and then to keep going until the business makes a profit. Usually the owner is the last to see any profit lining his pockets. Many times the owner goes into substantial debt just trying to get his or her business going.

SOLUTION #1

The Wade Cook method of investing in Covered Calls, Rolling Stock, stock options, dividends, spreads, buy-writes, rolling options, et cetera requires as little as $500 to get going. These methods generate a quick profit–again, actual cash, which can be pulled out and used, or be left alone to compound.

Most new businesses require a profound dedication and true commitment, and almost all businesses require extensive knowledge or experience. This brings me to problem number two.

PROBLEM #2 TIME/FINANCIAL COMMITMENT

Businesses are like babies–especially at first. They demand attention. You have to be there. Even when and *if* it grows, it requires more time to train and trust managers. It is hard to take vacations. It is difficult, but not impossible, to have a family life and/or a church life.

SOLUTION #2

The stock market, again the Wade Cook way, allows you to be as involved as you want. Most investors definitely "work" part-time. You control your time.

At one of my seminars, I started with this question: "How many of you want to make over $100,000 per year?" Hands shot up all over the classroom. Then I asked, "If you want to make over $100,000 per year, why are you talking to anyone about making money who is making less than that?" And then I continued, "To whom are you listening? Where are you getting your advice?"

You can probably relate to this question. You have probably kicked yourself for following the financial advice of people who "ain't makin' no money." Ironically, when you finish reading my chapters, you will probably ask some stockbroker (maybe even a well-known broker) whether you should buy my books and attend a Wall Street Workshop™. He or she will probably give you unintelligent advice. Please note that many of my students are stockbrokers who sit dazed and amazed at their former naivete. These students may have known bits and pieces before attending one of my Wall Street Workshops™, but no one, and I mean *no one*, has ever shown them how to systematically use a formula to generate perpetual income.

I have a background as a stockbroker and have been investing for about fifteen years. I thought I knew how to make money in the market, but I wasn't even close! The strategies taught [at the Wall Street Workshop™] really opened my eyes.

—NEIL W., PA

This seminar and Wade's books have filled in the gaps in my stockbroker education. As a stockbroker I learned how the markets work, but not how to personally make money. The firms I have worked for focus on selling (creating commission) and on customer service…not on learning strategies beyond buy and hold. Thanks for showing me what I was missing.

—DAVID S., TX

As a former stockbroker and current commodity broker, everything I ever wanted to do to help people make money in the markets was here at the Wall Street Workshop™. This is a dream come true for me and I can never truly explain how much of an impact was made on me today.

—RICHARD M., FL

I found this seminar extremely beneficial. I am a financial planner who works primarily in mutual funds and life insurance. Any financial professional who criticizes Wade's strategies is simply speaking out of ignorance. My practice with my clients will undoubtedly change in the future because of the results I personally have experienced.

-P. CHRISTOPHER M., OH

Your participation in your stock market business is only a few minutes at a time. You can read and study in your spare time (on airplanes, at lunch, in the bathroom, et cetera). A minimal amount of knowledge can be leveraged repetitiously to generate outstanding income. And you do not need a host of employees or managers to help you.

PROBLEM #3 OVERHEAD

With a traditional business you have rent, insurance, equipment, employees, taxes (FICA, employee withholding), phones, computers, even pencils and every other imaginable and unimaginable expense. The relentlessness of these expenses makes it difficult to make a profit on a continued basis. And it seems the amount of money needed to cover expenses rises to use up any available cash you have.

SOLUTION #3

This is where your business is very different. Simply put, you have none of these. Once you learn the Wade Cook formulas, you only buy stock or options and then sell them to generate a profit. If you currently have a brokerage account, it is easy to start investing, and there are many ways to make a profit (selling Covered Calls, Selling Puts, Rolling Options, et cetera) without having any overhead. When you make a profit, you keep it all. There are not a dozen strains or filters for your profits to go through, each one decreasing its size along the way, and all this before you get paid.

After two or three months of implementing these easy-to-use, but profound methods, most business entrepreneurs will be ecstatic. I know you will love the simplicity of it all.

The seminar was more than advertised. As a CPA, I found out how little I knew about obtaining wealth. Each strategy presented became more exciting. I am positive that I am finally on my way to becoming a millionaire.

—RAYMOND S., NY

I am a retired attorney, real estate broker, and financial planner who was looking for a new direction: something lucrative, but fun. This workshop has been everything I was looking for. Great instructor, with super knowledge and enthusiasm. I came here with great interest and am leaving a ball of fire. Is this fun or what! With the knowledge I have gained, and will gain with the Next Step™ and Wealth U™, my life has changed. Thank you

Wade Cook. As the second part of the Great Commandment says, "Thou shalt love thy neighbor as thyself." You are truly obeying that commandment.

—GEORGE R., UT

After 20 years of school with advanced degrees, I finally heard something that will actually work to both make and save money, and help with taxes and protection. The lecturers were fantastically knowledgeable, and had enough humor to make learning easy and pleasurable. They made it so you learned without knowing you learned.

—PAMELLA B., WA

PROBLEM #4 CAPITALIZING YOUR BUSINESS

Most businesses require a lot of start up money for buildings (rent, lease, purchase), product development, equipment, operating expenses, et cetera. They also require a large investment of time and energy, and most have a revenue curve that can take six months to two years to show any profit.

SOLUTION #4A

You can start in the stock market with almost nothing. Granted, if you start with less than a thousand dollars it is more difficult because the commissions eat up a large part of your smaller profits. But you surely don't need the amount of capital required to start up a traditional business.

SOLUTION #4B

Line of credit. I realize this part will not solve all your starting needs but "Margin Investing" is fun and it is definitely available. When you put $5,000 into your brokerage firm, your broker will let you borrow an additional $5,000 to buy stocks.

AN IMMEDIATE LINE OF CREDIT IS AVAILABLE.

This is a loan and the broker gets to choose the collateral (stocks they take). They will also charge interest on the outstanding balance (this is peanuts compared to the profits that can be generated).

You should be careful and pick stocks on dips, or stocks that will improve (use this amount for writing covered calls). If you make 22 to 38% per month, 7 to 9% interest a year is a small price to pay. (See margin variations and concerns in the *Wall Street Money Machine, Volume 1*.)

The solution to the second point listed above provides an interesting twist. Not only can you start your stock market cash flow business part time (even minutes a day), you can do this even when your existing business demands a lot of you. I use my car phone a lot. It allows me to be effective on the road and even when I travel.

Other interesting points:

1. Most people go into business for many reasons besides making money. They want to expand and grow, they want to develop and produce an idea, a product, or a service, and they want to not only control their destiny long term, but their time on a daily basis. Once in business they realize other people and other things control their time. They realize too late that most of their efforts are directed in ways which produce very little of their actual profits.

    They are quite delighted when they experience the simplicity of the methods of interfacing with the stock market (usually a phone call to their broker), the quick profits, and the end of the things that slow down the movement of income to the bottom line.

2. Investors can read and do research in the oddest places; driving around, in airplanes, while waiting, et cetera.

3. Investors can easily turn a getaway into a working vacation. Yes, you may need time away from your main business or job, but a few minutes here and there can really build up your stock market cash flow. Fifteen minutes a day could pay for your whole vacation and then some.

Problem #5 Specialized Knowledge

While it's true in your own business that you need a product or service and a certain degree of expertise in them, it's not exactly true in running your brokerage account.

Solution #5

1. Once you understand the Wade Cook system, learning and using specific formulas for cash flow generation, then you don't have to know everything about computer chips to invest in high tech stocks, or in temporary help companies to invest in them, et cetera. You learn the simple formulas and repetitive strategies, and find companies which fit the model. Your expertise is in the methods–working the formula, not in the stock.

2. As you start to invest for holding purposes–building your retirement portfolio–you can then get to be an expert in finding companies which are experts (specialists) in their own fields. You'll learn a lot about yields, what drives a stock, book value, earnings ratios, et cetera, as you move to this point.

    Note: I realize that someone hearing this for the first time may not understand this, so a very brief explanation is in order. I, Wade Cook, believe that at first an investor should employ a very aggressive approach to income generation. Proxy (low-cost, limited-risk options) trading allows an investor, by starting with a few thousand dollars, to build up to several hundred thousand in a year or two. I have too many students to count who have done this. It's exciting. Later you can take some profits, continue to do aggressive plays, but buy stocks which you like for the long haul. You can also take some profits and move them away from the market to buy real estate, second mortgages, CDs, annuities, et cetera. These have their own risk factors, but you are diversified.

3. If you have your own business, you probably know what it takes to be profitable, to expand and grow. This same knowledge can help you find in other companies the characteristics for success. For example: If you're a start up, you should know what it takes: look for Initial Public Offerings (IPOs). If you've

run your own business this will make sense. Use it to your best advantage.

Before I move off this topic, let me share a few more ideas.

Most businesses fail. Something like 80% of all new start-ups fail their first year. Of the 20% that make it, 80% of those fail the second year. That's a net of four or five businesses that make it. However, in franchising, 85% of franchisees make it their first year. Why? They have a track to run on, service and support, experience of the franchisor, combining the synergistic expertise of other franchisees, manuals, et cetera. The franchise fee and on-going fees are small prices to pay for good backup and support.

Stock Market Institute of Learning, Inc. has training, backup support, a clearinghouse of ideas, et cetera to help small investors, real estate investors, and small business people make a dramatic impact on their bottom line. If you don't use our training, please get it somewhere. Your first and then your continued and paramount investment should be in knowledge.

PROBLEM #6 WEALTH PROBLEMS
Once you start making good money you become a target for higher taxes, lawsuits and other risks.

SOLUTIONS #6
PROBLEM A: You need to learn how to reduce your exposure to risk and liability.

SOLUTION A: Set up a Nevada Corporation, Family Limited Partnership, and Charitable Remainder Trust.

PROBLEM B: You need to pay fewer taxes.

SOLUTION B: Attend Stock Market Institute of Learning's Wealth Institute. Set up a Nevada Corporation (even have a brokerage account in another state), a Charitable Remainder Trust, and a Pension Plan.

PROBLEM C: Make sure your family and church get everything.

SOLUTION C: Use a quality Family Living Trust in conjunction with other entities like a Charitable Remainder Trust (CRT).

Note: Call Stock Market Institute of Learning, Inc. at 1-800-872-7411 and ask about the B.E.S.T.™ (Business and Entity Skills Training which accompanies the Wall Street Workshop™) and our flagship event–the Wealth Institute.

> *The proper blending of these entities truly brings peace of mind.*

PROBLEM #7

Retiring at age 35 or being really cash flow rich at 65.

SOLUTION #7

Treat the stock market like a business. Buy wholesale, sell retail. Only buy so that you have something to sell. Be aggressive. The preceding methods are what my books and seminars are all about. Many people, starting with even $10,000, are ready to totally retire a year or two later. This is no joke. I say ready because they could if they wanted to but they're having too much fun. If you know you're going to make $5,000 today, it's pretty easy to get out of bed.

1. Do you invest in a pension type account?

    a. Keogh Plan for self employed,

    b. A Corporate Pension Plan,

    c. An IRA, SEP-IRA or Roth IRA.

Use peripheral entities for conducting the business or investments.

2. Many investments are "retirement" in nature.

    a. Annuities

    b. Real Estate

    c. Tax Advantaged Investments

All are deferred until you sell.

Training will help you determine which type is right and when it's right for you!

When a person is starting a business or in the midst of running or building up a business, his or her time demands are onerous.

Treating pension money like a business and doing aggressive strategies may be next to impossible. It may be difficult even putting money aside.

Two thoughts:

1. Do it anyway. Two-step the money away from your business. Discipline yourself to put money aside–the highest percentage (amount) possible even if you have to let it sit for awhile–invested in passive, "no hassle" investments.

2. Later when you slow down the "busyness" part of your life, then get more aggressive with your retirement money. Once you see how fast it compounds tax free you'll wish you had started earlier. The point: get rich in an account (entity) which pays no taxes. Don't put this off.

Remember you get a "double benefit" when you use a pension type arrangement.

1. Tax deductible donations–*investing with before-tax money.*

2. *All* income (dividends, interest, partnership, et cetera) and all capital gains are made tax free and compound tax free.

That's right, tax free–the pension plan pays no taxes. You only have to claim income in 30 to 40 years when you pull it out.

PROBLEM #8 INCLUDE FAMILY/TRAIN KIDS

An age-old problem exists in not only trying to involve your family but also in making sure they can perpetuate the dynasty.

SOLUTION #8

You'll have just as much problem here as in any business. Care, concern, legality, and dedication are time-honored problems.

1. A few solutions:

   a. Let your children manage a paper-trading account at first. Later let them use real money.

   b. Put money into an IRA for your kids to manage.

    c. Let them slowly take over the family accounts. (Set it up so they can only trade–not make withdrawals.)

    d. Let kids earn their way through college.

    e. Discuss strategies frequently and assign research projects.

    f. Have them visit companies and ask questions.

    g. Immerse them in reading–articles, stories, reports, news releases.

    h. Plan working vacations–visit factories, companies (many will give tours).

    i. Attend shareholder meetings.

    j. Track the impact of:
- New products and services
- Competition
- Expansion
- Acquisition of debt, mergers
- Share buybacks
- Stock splits

    k. Take them to seminars, forums, et cetera. Call Stock Market Institute of Learning, Inc. about the Youth Wall Street Workshop™.

    l. Listen to them. Let them ask their questions and let their questions guide you.

2. More thoughts for older kids:

I believe the best financial gift a mother and father can leave is instilling in their children a desire to be self-sufficient, a team player, passionate, and willing to do "what it takes" to support their families. If the parents are rich and have older children, they eventually need to be brought into the family dynasty–either to dismantle it or perpetuate it. All of the thoughts given above for younger children apply to your 40 and 60 year old children–most adults are teenagers when it comes to wealth protection and wealth endowment.

PROBLEM #9 WINDING DOWN YOUR BUSINESS

Sometimes it is more difficult to end a business than it is to start. You may have employees, leases, contracts, and commitments. It can be painful.

SOLUTION #9

Stock market investing has no such demands. The worst "hard to get out of" situation you could get into would be a stock or mutual fund which is currently down in value.

Some thoughts:

1. If you follow the Wade Cook system, your emphasis will have been on cash flow. Retiring will mean doing less or putting your extensive profits into high yielding investments or Section 29 income and utility stocks, bonds, MIPS, et cetera for income and tax credits.

2. The activity of building your fortunes will now help you choose wise investments. If you have been using careful forethought, you will have used some of your profits to purchase high quality stocks. Quitting will not be painful but a smooth transition many months or years in the making. You will learn how to build a solid financial house with a good supporting foundation.

PROBLEM #10 DRIVE AND PASSION—FUN AND EXCITEMENT

Rarely have I seen a true entrepreneur go into business for the "money" alone. They want to help to contribute to others and to better their family's position. Most humans know instinctively that the way to wealth is to enlarge the pie. The problem is many get bogged down, dismayed, and even after decades feel unsatisfied.

SOLUTION #10

The stock market will not solve this last problem. The proper application of knowledge is exciting. Working and fine-tuning cash flow formulas will produce pronounced results. Involving family and friends can be gratifying. Preparing for a great retirement is thrilling. Planning your financial affairs so your family, church, or charity get everything is satisfying. Ultimately, your true happiness will come down to your relationship between you and your Maker.

It is to this ultimate end that we at Stock Market Institute of Learning, Inc. dedicate our service to you and hope that we are but one stepping stone to help your sojourn on this earth be one of peace, happiness and fulfillment.

3

EARNING MONEY

That portion of your portfolio you've chosen to use as your cash generation machine should be used wisely, yet aggressively as you see fit.

You need to find your comfort level and then trade within that level. As you gain more experience, you'll probably spread the edge of the envelope–try new things, or variations. This chapter is about several of these other ways of making money. However, in order to put this information in such a way you can easily use it, this chapter is like a "play sheet," or a checklist. It will cover most of my formulas in an abbreviated format. I'll try to be complete with the quantity, but brief with the explanation. Indeed, I'll try to keep the definition or explanation to one or two paragraphs.

Each of these formulas is explained in detail in other books, primarily in *Wall Street Money Machine, Volume 1*, and *Volume 4*, (formerly titled *Safety 1st Investing*), other home study courses, primarily *Zero to Zillions* and *Red Light, Green Light*, and in other reports I write as I perfect various strategies.

I wish more than anything that when I started investing I would have had a chapter like this–to see in a few pages all the potential plays, formulas and recipes.

So here we go. We'll start with my old favorite. Remember, these strategies are about generating predictable cash flow.

ROLLING STOCK

There are certain stocks that trade within a certain range. Some brokers call this channeling. They move up to a high (resistance) and then to a low (support). Many stocks do this, but the ones I like (so I don't have a lot of cash tied up) are cheaper stocks–say in the $1 to $5 range. I find a stock which goes from $2 to $2.75. It doesn't seem like a lot of profit, but 75¢ on a $2 investment in one to three or four months is not bad. Look at the following examples:

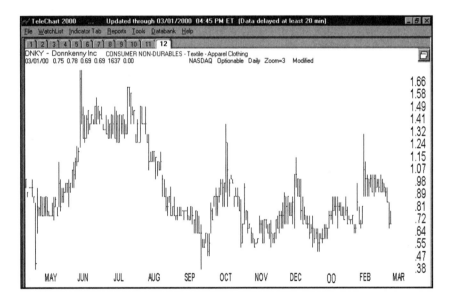

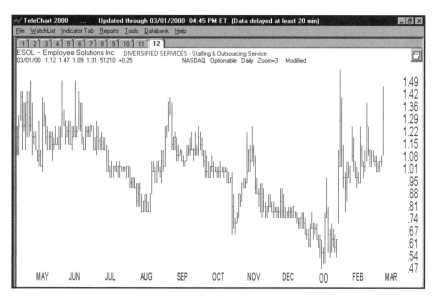

The three rules of rolling stocks are:

1. You always know your exit before you go in the entrance.

2. Don't get greedy–sell below the high for quicker and surer profits.

3. Stick with the less expensive stocks–so you can buy more.

Many high-priced stocks roll. Look at the following:

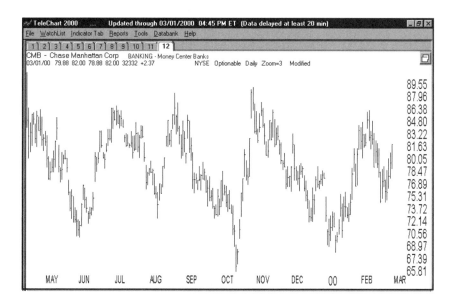

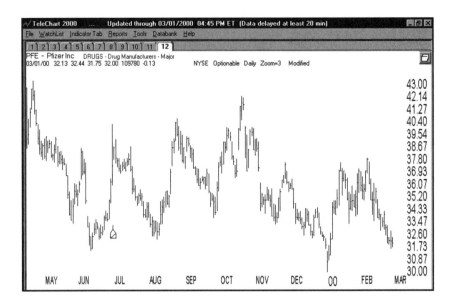

These are nice predictable rolls, but they are high priced. I play them, but with options. See the section on Rolling Options.

BOTTOM FISHING

This is a simple way of finding stocks which are severely underpriced, or at least ones which you think have a high likelihood for going much higher.

Stocks in this category could come from:

1. Really bad news.

2. Bankrupt (Chapter 11) companies on their way out of bankruptcy.

3. Turnarounds.

4. Companies just going public or just getting listed on an exchange.

5. Companies breaking out of their roll range with better earnings, new products, et cetera.

6. Traditional penny stocks with some reason (pressure) for the stock to go up.

I do bottom fishing stocks all the time. I bought 141,500 shares of one company at around 6¢ and sold it 18 months later for $1.40 to $1.50. A nice $200,000 profit! I look for more opportunities like this all the time.

Oh, by the way. I was seriously challenged in this statement by one of our Big Brother government agencies. Too bad this did happen in 1994 with a stock ticker symbol IDID (Comparator Systems Corp.) to make the scenario complete. I'll put the details here.

I found out about this from a student at one of our superb live Wall Street Workshops™. I love going to these events. I learn something new every time. The company trading symbol was IDID.

I purchased 141,500 shares at an average price of .055¢. My total investment was $7,893.86. About 15 months later I sold the stock for $1.47, $1.53, and $1.50, and grossed $209,170. My net profit after costs including commissions was $196,919. So I made more in less time than my government detractors hoped to find.

The sad part is that many people found out about this obtrusive meddling. Just the word "investigate" causes fear. It seems everyone believes the allegations, but nobody believes the defense or rebuttal. Thousands upon thousands of students have benefited greatly by learning, and employ our safety first, conservative cash flow formulas. I'm saddened for the ones who haven't attended the Wall Street Workshop™ because of the statements of a few wrong-headed and bungling bureaucrats.

DIVIDENDS

I also like to share in the profits of the company. I take all the dividends I can take, but for the most part I'd rather the company keep the profits and expand the business.

These dividends include regular dividends, irregular dividends (which I look for all the time), a cash distribution (which may not be taxable, but which reduces the price of the stock which could be sold for a loss), and MIPS, or Monthly Income Preferred Securities–large companies which pay out monthly checks.

One of my strategies is to own the stock long enough (sometimes as little as one day) to capture the dividend. Wait until it increases in value, and then sell it.

OPTIONS

Buying stock options gives the investor a chance to control large amounts of stocks with a small amount of money. An option gives you the right (not the obligation) to buy or sell a stock. Because options end–they expire–they are very risky. If you learn how to play them well, the profits can be phenomenal. I've written extensively on many forms of option investing elsewhere, so only a brief synopsis is here.

Call Options: A right to buy stock. You buy these when you think the stock is going up. This could be on a SLAM (serious down movement), a roll (when the stock is at the bottom of the roll range), or a stock with good news, et cetera. In short, when you think the stock has pressure to move up, buy a call, ride it up, and sell.

Put Options: A right to sell stock. You build value in your put option as the stock decreases. Buy puts when the stock hits a high, or is at the top of its roll range, in short, when you think the high price can't be sustained.

Rolling Options: Buying calls or selling puts when a stock is at its low range and then buying a put, or selling a call, when it peaks out and starts back down. Look at the following:

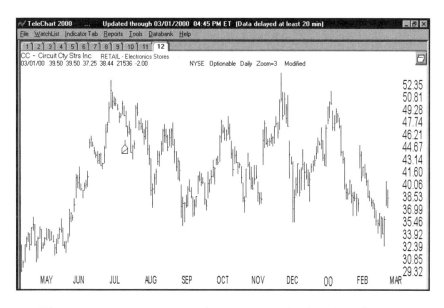

This gives you a way to make money on both sides of the movement.

Sell Calls–Covered: Writing covered calls is one of my favorite ways to generate consistent cash flow. Yes, there are other ways I make more money, but not as consistently. This method lets you generate income (in one day) by selling a call option on stock you already own or stock you've purchased for just this purpose.

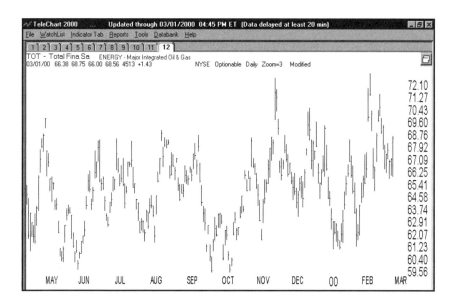

The rules include:

1. Buy stock on margin–this allows you to double your rate of return.

2. Volatility–almost like a rolling stock so we can take advantage of the swings.

3. Keeping within the $5 to $25 price range for maximum returns with a small amount of cash tied up.

There are many variations, techniques, and examples found in my other books. One awesome variation is the Lazy A and Lazy B Covered Call. I put out a seminar in an update CD format (It is just $10. Call 1-800-872-7411). This is definitely worth learning about. It will help you generate a steady 20% monthly return.

As the stock moves down, the price of the options moves down also. In writing covered calls, we either sell the call (uncovered–if we don't own the stock) or buy the stock (hopefully at the low) and wait to sell the call as the stock increases. We want maximum cash flow so we sell at the "maximum" time.

We bought the stock at $4 and sold the $5 call (about 35 days away–the next month) for $1.25 when the stock was $4.87. At the time we bought the stock, the $5 call was 12.5¢. We take advantage of the stock movement, hence compounding the option rate of return.

Uncovered calls: Many of you won't be able to do this until you have more experience and/or more cash in your account. This is called "going naked," in that you don't own the stock. You use this strategy when the stock is at the high part of its range. You sell the call–generating pure cash. You wait. As the stock moves down, your obligation to deliver (sell) the stock goes down and eventually disappears as the time expires. You make money with no investment. You will, however, have to hold between 30 to 50% of the stock value in your account–this is the margin requirement and it differs from firm to firm. The risk is that if the stock goes up, you'll have to buy it at a higher price (offset by the cash you made for selling the call). Don't sell calls on stocks you think are going up; either buy the stock low (covered) and wait to sell the call–getting a higher premium for the options and eventually selling (getting called out) at a higher price, or sell the call when the stock is high–wait for a dip and then:

1. Buy the stock or

2. Buy back the option or

3. Just let the option expire and keep the cash!

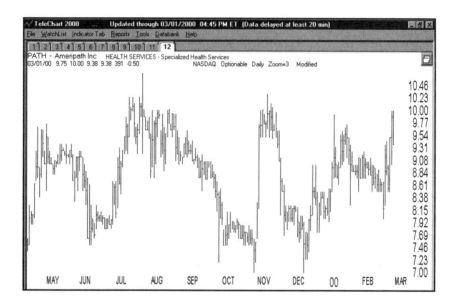

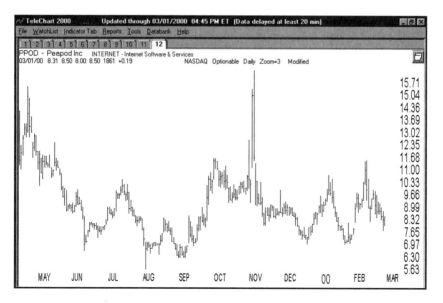

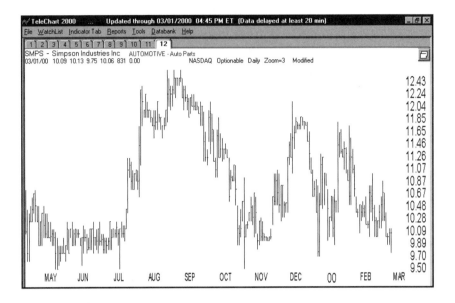

Selling Puts: This is a great way to make money. You sell a put, generating income. You are selling the right for someone to put (sell) the stock to you at a fixed price. You use this strategy when the stock is low and heading up. The income (premium) you received is yours to keep. As the stock rises, the put option you sold goes down in value. You could either buy back the option at a lower price and keep the difference, or let it lapse on the expiration date. If the stock has risen above the strike price, no one will put it to you. If you do have to buy the stock, the cost is offset by the premium received–like buying whole-sale.

Spreads: There are many combinations, but my favorite is a combination of buying/selling calls and/or buying/selling puts on the same stock simultaneously. Here is how it works.

SCENARIO

Stock low, going up. Do a bull put spread. Say Microsoft dips to $96 and you think it's heading back up. Sell the $95 put and buy the $90 put. You have created a $5 spread. If you did 10 contracts this would be $5,000. If you sold the $95 put for $4, or $4,000 and purchase the $90 put for $2\frac{1}{8}$, or $2,125, you would net $1,875. You have limited downside risk, or $5,000 minus the $1,875, or $3,125, meaning that if the stock tanks you can only lose $3,125. If the stock stays above

$95 on the expiration–the third Friday of next month (even if it dips below $95 briefly)–you'll keep the $1,875. $3,125 on hold (margin) and at risk to make $1,875 is a cool profit.

Only do bull put spreads when you're bullish on a stock.

Note: Another bullish strategy is the bull call spread. I like these (especially in the Lazy B Covered Call), but it's a debit spread, thus requiring a second set of commissions as you end the trade. Debit spreads cost money. Credit spreads make money–actually you take in money when you put the trade in place and keep it if the trade goes your way.

SCENARIO

Stock high, going down. Do a bear call spread. A bear call spread is a credit spread and is easy to implement. Remember if the stock is high, one play is to sell calls–even naked (not owning the stock). The problem is most readers will not be allowed to do this and the margin requirements are hefty. The risk is that the stock will run up so you would have to deliver the stock (get paid) at a lower price than the stock cost! Let's say just before earnings a stock runs up $20 from $110 to $130. It's at an all time high. It has great earnings, announced after the market close, and it spikes up $13 at the open. You feel the price can't be sustained. You've made a nice profit on the $110 calls you purchased last week, but now its time to ride it down. You could buy puts, but you remember there is only a one in three chance of making money when you buy calls or puts. The stock (hence the options) has to perform as you wish. However, by selling something you have a two in three chance of making money–probably a three in three chance– you sell the $145 call. Wow, they're going for $8 and there's only ten days left to expiration. Your risk is that the stock goes above $145 and you get called out. Then to lessen this risk–yes, actually cap it–and to seriously reduce the 30 to 50% margin requirement, buy the $150 call. Oh, oh. They are $6. That $8,000 profit is now reduced to $2,000 because you've spent $6,000 on insurance.

You've created a $5,000 spread. Your credit is a net of $2, or $2,000. Your risk is $3,000 ($5,000 minus the credit of $2,000). Your hold or margin is really the whole $5,000, but someone (the marketplace) gave you the $2,000, so it's just $3,000 of your own money. If the stock runs up to $160, you could lose all or part of your $3,000. You can always unwind the spread for a partial loss.

If the stock stays below $145, you're just fine. You get to keep the $2,000 with no further obligation or expense. A nice 60% return for two weeks.

Note: I've written extensively on this strategy in *Wall Street Money Machine, Volume 4: Safety 1st Investing*. Also, I've created a whole new video home study course of my one-day Spread & Butter™ seminar. It sells for $350,000 and worth every penny of it. Sometimes it's on sale for $1,695. Call 1-800-872-7411 and ask if there are, or will be, any specials in this millennium.

When the stock is low, sell a put and buy a call—both strategies gain advantage with an increase in the stock price. You make money now selling the put, and you make more later selling the call option you purchased.

When the stock is high, sell a call and buy a put. You make money on each as the stock moves down. This gives you four plays on a rolling stock with options.

Short Selling: Short selling allows you to borrow stock, sell it, and generate income. As the stock moves down, you purchase it, pay off the loan (borrowed stock), and pocket the difference. It's easier said than done, but in my case, I'd rather buy puts or do bear call spreads if I think the stock is going down. I use short selling when I've sold a naked call and have to perform. I'll borrow stock to cover my position and hope it turns down.

Blue Chips: There are so many definitions of blue chips that you need to make up your own definition. These are the stocks you want to own for a long time. They could be brand name stocks, large companies that have fallen out of favor, even regional companies you can identify with.

CASH FLOW

Use your profits from selling stocks and options for investing in real estate or other businesses, or put your money into good, solid blue chip stocks. The name of the game is to use your stock market profits to buy your "hold" investments.

You choose the percentage or amount of your money that you want to put to work to generate income. Turn the stock market into your own business—your own cash flow machine.

4

QUICK TURN PROFITS

I wrote my first book almost two decades ago. I have had a wonderful audience–a very supportive following. Those of you who know how I write and think will definitely be unsettled by the following chapter!

There is a purpose, a rhyme, and reason to my madness. Indeed, it is in my attempt to explain my "stock market madness" that the following is written. Why? People come up and ask me how I can make such fantastic returns. How do I consistently get huge cash amounts?

For example, listed below are our returns for 1999. I hope you do much better. This is with a rather large amount of money. Many people get better returns then this on smaller amounts because they can "tend the garden" better.

WADE COOK FINANCIAL CORPORATION
ALL BROKERAGE ACCOUNTS
YEAR ENDED 12/31/1999
Audited

RATE OF RETURN RESULTS

Wade Cook Financial Corporation*   127.59%

   *Includes all realized and unrealized gains/losses

AVERAGE IN BROKERAGE ACCOUNTS (MONTHLY)

Wade Cook Financial Corporation $2,917,816

REALIZED/UNREALIZED GAINS

Wade Cook Financial Corporation $3,722,950
   Realized Gains $3,255,750
   Unrealized Gains $467,190

These are pretty spectacular results. And to put it in perspective, this $3,722,950 is not (a) an increase from the average monthly amount in the account. It is the actual profits of the account. It truly is a 127% gain. And it is not (b) some ambiguous, nebulous number, or "unrealized gain." Part of the $3,722,950 is unrealized ($467,190), but $3,255,750 is actual cash profits.

Now, we realize this is quite embarrassing to the big guys, especially all of those who have criticized me so incessantly. Also, to my *"Big Brother is watching"* friends, we continue to invite your queries and your comments. We think state and federal agencies should make our courses mandatory, so more people can learn these basic cash flow formulas, learn to work better with their financial professionals, and then keep their money out of harms way. *Wall Street Money Machine, Volume 4: Safety 1st Investing*, outlines and explains these basic protective techniques.

I'll get back to you and what you can do and how you can accomplish consistent monthly "cash flow." Before that, let me explain a few things, basically laying out how you will be able to beat my returns at certain times.

So, to my wonderful critics I say, "Eat your heart out," and again, you can find all these trades on Wealth Information Network™ at www.wadecook.com.

So come along–I hope you'll come to understand my rationale and my results. It will take a while, but the first part of this chapter is necessary to understand the last part, the crucial part. It may be slow at first, and you'll have to wade through my "Wade-isms," as I have never before tried to encapsulate this thinking process and results. This is new territory. Hopefully not the final frontier.

HOLY MACRO

I hope to give a "macro-view" and use micro examples to justify my reasoning. There definitely is a "herd" mentality and I am not the first one to try to understand it and to figure out how to profit from it, or how to not lose by following it. More importantly, trying to understand this type of stock market mentality is the perfect way to try to figure out just when the "herd" is about to turn. This turning point is the point when a lot of profits can be made. But I'm ahead of myself. That is the conclusion to this chapter. The profit-making point of reversal or correction of a stock is crucial. I bring it up at the beginning so you know where this chapter is heading. I will not be untrue to the theme that has worked well for me, both in my personal investing and my seminars: use a little cash to purchase an asset, get in, then get out with a nice chunk of cash (profits) or smaller cash flows (payments). In short, I want income (cash flow) from dividends, capital gains, option premiums, or whatever income that allows us to live, to pay the bills, and grow rich.

Another theme of my books and seminars is "to whom are we listening?" If you want to make $100,000 a year, why are you listening to anyone making under $100,000 a year? It is to this point that we'll launch into this area of discussion.

There is a widespread belief that the market is always right. I disagree. There are too many variables. The market is not always right. When it comes to a particular stock, there is definitely too much sentiment to come to any conclusion that a stock's price is "right." (I'll give in on this a little, if you're determining a stock price based on a "best guess" midpoint price between a high and a low, or a recent support level and resistance level.)

I'll get back to individual stocks later, but for now let's deal with the stock market in general.

COMMON BELIEFS

Supply and Demand. There is a common "wish" that all things be simple and easy to explain. Do markets move due to a supply and a demand? Yes, to an extent, but there is too much sentiment, too many desires, and far too many biases which come into play.

MARKET SENTIMENT

When you have sentimental responses to hard facts, you are bound to get a distortion. Those who believe in equilibrium or that the market is a zero-sum game are often fooled. A fund manager may make a clever play one day, but then be hoisted on his own petard the next.

Market sentiment is a combination of multiple dynamics at work. If we were to achieve perfect knowledge, have perfect competition, and perfect responses to all this, and more importantly, if we could be detached from the game, then maybe we could pre-guess a movement. But we get nothing perfect and we are not detached. Indeed, we are a part of the course of events.

When we buy stocks, we're part of the process that drives the stock up; when we sell, we are the opposite. The amount of stock movement depends on where the market is headed—what stage, or cycle it is in.

INFLUENCE

We, individually, have little influence, but collectively we have a lot. If we are in the game, buying a stock or many stocks, we contribute. We become part of the trend. We want safety so we go with the numbers—the "herd."

This has never made sense to me—as most of the stock market makes no sense to me. I love "crazy!" Since I accumulate wealth through chaos—at least, figuring out part of the chaos and capturing profits amidst it, and since I don't have to continue in the trend, in fact I can be detached from it (as you can)–then you and I can make incredible returns.

MR. SPOCK, WHERE ARE YOU?

If you think the stock market is logical, or that a certain move in a particular stock price is logical, then I will show you dozens of illogical moves! Can you predict a price change–100% of the time? No. Can you do your best to make a calculated risk? Yes.

Try this one on for size. When a stock price starts to rise, it creates excitement. The higher it goes (or the faster the rise) the more investors want in on the action. It rises more. More investors buy in. It rises and rises, sometimes 10 to 20% in a few days. Then…it stops! Does it just stay there? Or does it swing back down? Usually it falls as investors' sentiment takes it the other way.

I'll give a five-step process in a while, but first, what is happening here? Which price was right–the price two weeks ago at $80 a share, or the price now at $120? And three weeks from now, what will be right? The $90 price which the stock has fallen back to, the $80, or high of $120?

What did supply and demand have to do with this? What about the market always being right, a search for equilibrium, or any other high-falutin' theory exposed by the gurus of Wall Street? Maybe, just maybe, this $30 run up was because a competitor's Indonesia mining operation turned sour. But look what the "herd" did!

Here's another one. Throughout this past year employment reports have been good–more people employed. To me this should be good news. It means more people working, paying taxes, and not living off the government. It means more savings, more spending, and all the other great things that help make a bigger American pie.

But, no. The stock market (DJIA) falls 80 points. Why? Because, as those wonderful things happen, inflation will go up, then the Feds, in nine months or a year, will edge up interest rates; corporate profits will decline slightly in 12 to 18 months, so the stock prices will fall. But they fall now in anticipation of this chain of events–which no one can predict anyway.

I rest my case for craziness. However, this last point does make a nice segue to a discussion of future events.

PERFECTING THE FUTURE

Markets rise and fall on a perception of what will happen in the future. I have two problems with this.

1. No one knows what will happen. Too many other things change. What seems logical turns illogical.

2. We still must take into account our biases—how we as individuals and groups view such things. Life is too fluid to predict.

Most of the future's news is discounted long before it happens. Look at the last example! We want to discern things, to have peace of mind, to have things fit—to make sense. What twisted logical path did the market (the invisible "they") walk down to come to a conclusion that a stock's price will fall in nine to eighteen months, and then have the price fall now? With this type of logic at work and the crazy reaction to it, what are we to do? More importantly, what plays can we make to build up our income?

I'll give specifics in a few moments, but first, my list of important observations:

1. Individual Investors

    a. There is in each of us (even at the corporate level) a desire to grow, to build, to achieve.

    b. We all, even companies, have a desperate need to not only survive, but to thrive.

2. Market Movement

    a. The market has a mind of its own and will usually do that which it must do to make fools out of a majority of investors.

    b. The market is not right. It just isn't. It's fluid and moves unexpectedly.

    c. There are short-term plays and long-term plays—you decide the length of time.

    d.   There are opportunities everywhere.

    e.   Investors' actions shape future events, not predict them. They cause change, not reflect it.

    f.   Investor bias rationalizes (and hence changes) the facts.

    g.   You can profit going both ways–up prices, and down prices.

    h.   The "herd" mentality takes over and when it's played out (the boom), then prices start down as they bottom out (the bust). Then the cycle starts over.

    i.   It is at this precise moment when you capitalize on profits.

It took a lot to get to these points, so let's keep rolling. Let's use a stock moving up for whatever reason as our example. We own a stock or have an option on it. The stock moves with a mind of its own. It's reflective of news–good earnings, higher dividend paid out, prospects for the next few years. Everyone wants in. The price goes up and up. However, it will turn around to some degree. The sentiment will change.

The time comes when the momentum will turn. Perhaps the turn will come when an analyst at a major firm, a person who has loved this stock (to death!), now thinks it shouldn't be an "aggressive buy," but a "buy," or a "hold." A small downgrade. If you are into buying puts or going short on the stock, wouldn't it be great to sell at the peak, or buy the puts just as the stock is about to fall?

This is it. We can play this high point and the corresponding reverse (bottom) point. And, it's just not that tough to make money this way. We'll call this point a "crossover," or a convergence. Crossovers occur at both peaks and valleys.

We'll explore this premise after we look at a scenario. This scenario conforms to this strategy. Not all scenarios do, but the ones which do allow us to get in, then get out with a lot of cash. This scenario plays out frequently; I'm not investing in "the market," but in certain stocks and options within the general market. And if you think the market has a mind of its own, go with the trend. Don't try to "catch a falling piano." Only go with the trend so far.

FIVE SECTIONS (STAGES) OF A CROSSOVER (THE BOOM/BUST SCENARIO)

1. The price movement is unnoticeable. The trend starts, the price rises or falls inordinately quickly compared to its historical moves. Volume increases as stock momentum builds. Look at the following:

QUALCOM (QCOM)

December, 1998, the stock had been trading between $10 to $20 for several months. Volume increased in QCOM in March and April, 1999 and the stock started to climb. The stock split at the end of December, and has been trading between $125 and $140 for a couple of months.

AT HOME (ATHM)

At Home showed a big trend up in late 1998 and early 1999. At Home then showed a trend reversal in April 1999. The trend continued to the downside until November, when it made an unsuccessful attempt to change back into an uptrend.

2. Activity reinforces more activity. Recommendations (from the professionals) fly. Everyone wants in. Major purchases occur.

APPLE COMPUTER (AAPL)

Apple has shown a good uptrend starting in April 1999. During the downturn in September, the stock volume decreased until the trend changed back to the upside in October, 1999.

3. The strength (or weakness) is tested. Doubts occur in the wisdom of the recommendation. New recommendations appear, after all the facts are used, distorted and abused to prove points.

4. The main point, or question, is simple—is the price sustainable?

   a. Where is the market headed?

   b. Check other news.

   c. How was the news received?

   d. How much buying has been going on?

   e. How many institutions jumped in?

   f. When the high and low was tested, did the price return to the previous support level or did it break support?

5. Divergence. If there is no compelling reason for it to stay high, it will decline. *But if there is no compelling reason for a fall,* it may fluctuate, but the stock might establish a new range. The price will be tested repeatedly. The opposite is true for a falling stock once it hits bottom. The bottom support level will be tested repeatedly.

A PERSPECTIVE

Go with the "herd" until the time is right. Buck the trend at that time. I have seen very rapid movements up and down. I hope after this next sentence or two my strategy will make sense. So much doesn't make sense, but this does. The stock price will change.

If I own a stock at $80 and it gets trendy–caught in an updraft, I'd rather sell at $110–even if it goes to $120, because in two hours it could fall to $90, or a $50 stock could fall to $35. *A good time to get out would be when you wouldn't get in.*

UP ELEVATORS/DOWN ELEVATORS

Here is a micro point on these movements. I think good news plays out in days. However, it can take months for company's stock prices to recover from bad news.

Now, if you're playing the stock, either long or short, the length of time is crucial to your profitability. However, if you're playing stock options, a high point and then a small percentage down in the stock, or a bottom and small recovery in the stock ($1 to $5) could produce drastic profits.

DEFINE A JOKE

Watching "Data" on Star Trek is a lesson in human behavior. Laughing (getting a joke) is difficult–at least the timing is difficult. Data doesn't get jokes. He can't tell one, or understand the punchline. I saw a bad movie (Solo) and the humanoid (machine) questioned why everyone was laughing. "A joke," he was told. Obviously, he wants to know what a joke is. No good explanation was given. Let me try my hand at it. I'll then get back to booms and busts. A joke is a story, and at the end a complete surprise occurs, either in the actions of the participants, or a twist in words, with unexpected meaning, hidden meaning, or a nuance to something else. Based on your point of reference, the company you're in, or the mood you're in, determines your response–a chuckle, a scoff, or a belly laugh, et cetera.

It is the twist or reversal that interests me. Never has a movie brought tears to my eyes as the end of *Steel Magnolias*–then in a half second everyone is busting a gut laughing. The writer played our emotions like a maestro. The markets also thrive on fear and greed, and unexpected reversals.

CHANGE IS INEVITABLE

When stocks move up or down–either unexpectedly or in reaction to news, especially if they move quickly, there is a high incidence of a major divergence. A favorite play is to buy a call or do a bull put spread on the low-side turnaround, and buy a put or do a bear call spread on the top-side turnaround (*Note:* See *Wall Street Money Machine, Volume 4,* formerly titled *Safety 1ˢᵗ Investing,* for more information on spreads.)

A perception of the facts (right or wrong) starts the movement. Activity breeds activity and more investors rush in. They listen to current events and future predictions that subsequently affect the price. Their purchasing/selling is integral to the process. New information–either right or wrong–tests the strength or weakness of the previous assumption/activity, and the price is sustained or divergence occurs. A short-term profit can be made. It's quick and semi-predictable. Get in and out before anyone ever sees (or reacts to) the trend.

Now, use your profits to increase your holdings in great companies. It is the very *boom and bust cycle* (volatility) that gets me excited. Most investors run from the boom and bust scenario. However, some of us profit big time from this technique.

5

FUN-DAMENTALS

Ⓘf there is a way to make the selection of a stock and building a portfolio of solid stocks a fun process, we'll make every attempt to find it. A few assumptions: 1) we want to find stocks at bargain prices, and 2) we surely do not want to overpay for our stocks.

Isn't that the essence of it all–to find great stocks at bargain prices? Also, we want to buy stocks with the highest likelihood to increase in value and the lowest likelihood of losing value. If the stock produces a dividend (income) that would be nice too.

Real Estate: A Foundational Example
Determining value is very perplexing and very difficult. Over the years many ways of determining value have been proposed. Whether we're buying or selling, we want the best price. The three most common ways to determine real estate value are listed here. After this short exploration we'll use what's applicable from this to aid us in choosing stocks.

COST OR REPLACEMENT VALUE

Buildings and land have value based on how it is being used. We'll explore more of this in the income section, but we'll cover it briefly here. A building used as a factory will be worth so much: use it for residences and it may go up in value. Turn it into a shopping center and it goes up again. You can't do this with stock, but what the company does with its assets can change what it's worth.

With real estate we just figure what it costs to replace the building—including the land—and that's the replacement cost. Is it this simple? Well—not quite.

INCOME

The gross and net income and the use of income multipliers are the most commonly used basis for the determination of value. You see, the cost of replacing a structure is not adequate to determine the full or accurate value.

What income does a building make? And even if you know that to the penny, other factors enter in:

1. How long has it been since a rent increase?

2. How expensive is the debt? And can it be refinanced or paid off?

3. Can other expenses be lowered?

And none of this has to do with tax deductions. How does it affect our tax bracket? All sorts of other variations occur. If we raise the rents, will the income remain stable? If we "net" more, the value will increase—could it be refinanced at a higher price and the new-found money used to buy more properties?

"COMPS"

One common way to value real estate is to find properties in the area which have sold recently and determine the value of your property based on an average of several properties—taking into account the differences. This is one of the functions of appraisers. Banks use this method extensively so they are not giving mortgages above "what the neighborhood will bear."

Extensive appraisals can be done using all three of these methods. It is wise to use all three with a more nebulous "growth potential" factor thrown in. The potential for growth or increase in value is a reason why many real estate investors invest in the first place, but so many things change, and there are so many chances to be wrong, that hardly anyone uses it as a main factor in determining current value.

I could go on, but since this is a chapter about stocks, let's just take from real estate the thought behind the process. The example of real estate cannot solve all the problems, or answer all the questions, but it is worthwhile. It's good to have another point of reference. I'm good at many of my stock decisions because I integrate knowledge I gained in real estate.

The point is not that many companies own real estate, but that the price of the stock, the income, and tax consequences have many similar characteristics.

Now, To Stocks

There are five major areas to look at in determining the value of a stock. There are several minor aspects and variations that can also be examined. No one of these should stand alone. You will get a "five blind men and the elephant" view if you do so. Also, there is no set "weighting" exercise that I've found. In the end it comes down to your feelings and the risk you're willing to take; the direction you want to go.

Fundamental analysis is different than technical analysis. Technical analysis uses charts to identify significant market trends or specific stock turns. The use of technical analysis, like fundamental analysis, is to help reduce risk.

Technical analysis' most useful function is to help confirm a movement that seems unrealistic, too hopeful, or even unpopular. Charts tell us things like a doctor does—what is the past history, the diagnosis, the chances, and the effect of certain factors like diet or exercise.

This section is about fundamental analysis. I read the technical books, study their methods, and I use what I understand, but pure numbers have never had that much appeal to me. I like the challenge of figuring out movements, values—entrance and exit points. While I love technical information, I also love the basics, the fundamentals. I use both, but ultimately base my decisions on my own "gut feeling" after looking at all the data I can collect.

The main reason I favor the fundamental approach is that all movements have their genesis in one or more of the fundamental aspects of the stock. Fundamental approaches take a "separate" or a dispassionate look at the stock (or the market). Technical aspects of movements are not apart from, but integral to the stock or the market movements. Fundamentals give people opinions, while technicals try to confirm those opinions.

Whichever method you favor, trying to predict the future movement is the goal, and trying to reduce risk along the way in order to forecast these movements is what separates winners from losers. Yes, there is risk, but you know you can't get something for nothing. Risk is the price you pay for the rewards.

The following fundamentals are the five main methods or tools to help you make good decisions, to hit a lot of singles and a few homers, all the while trying to avoid too many strike outs.

EARNINGS

We will first discuss earnings and earnings per share, or P/E. The earnings of a company are its bottom line—they are the profits (after taking out dividends to shareholders of any preferred stock and after taxes).

To figure the earnings per share, we take the number of shares outstanding and divide it into earnings—hence we get earnings per share. *Earnings are very important* and are that which the company uses for dividend payouts, for investment in growth, for excess debt reduction. This figure is most often used by lending institutions for calculation of new debt paybacks.

Earnings should be from sales, and not from one-time phenomenons like the sale of a division, or a bad investment charge off. Many sources list earnings per share: *Barron's, Investor's Business Daily*, most local newspapers with financial information, and most computer on-line services.

In determining your stock purchases, you'll not only want current figures, but you'll want to know where the company has been. Does it have a history of increasing earnings? Did they increase, then slow down? You need to understand why the earnings per share are what they are.

The P/E is a very important number. I teach this from coast to coast. "When in doubt," I say, "follow earnings." Yes, the other measuring sticks are useful, but not as important as earnings. Think of it. Some companies just don't need a lot of assets to produce income. Some need a lot of assets and other forms of overhead.

The P/E is stated in terms that let us figure how much each dollar of our stock purchase is making. If the company's stock is trading at $80 and it earns $8 per share, it has a multiple of 10. If it's making $4 per share, it has a multiple, or P/E of 20; 20 times $4 equals $80. Another way would be to divide $4 into $80 and get 20, or a P/E of 20. In this case, what we're saying as investors is that we are willing to accept a 5% cash flow return (even though we may not actually receive the $4 or the $8); 5% of $80 is $4.

As I've said, P/Es are very, very important. We need to understand how to use them–and how to keep them in perspective.

To decide if a P/E for a particular company is good, we need to: 1) pick a number we're happy with–say, "I'll buy any company with a P/E under 24," or 2) compare it to the market as a whole, or 3) compare it to stocks in the same sector, say high-tech or pharmaceuticals.

Let's look at 2), as 1) is self-explanatory. Standard and Poors has an index of 500 stocks. It's called the S&P 500. The combined P/E for these companies is in the thirties. You compare your company to this number and get a feel for how well it's doing.

You could also look at a smaller picture and compare your stock to other companies in the same business. There are so many variables in trying to get a handle on this information. One problem is that different reporting services use different time periods. For example, one newspaper may use "trailing 12 months" numbers to figure a company's P/E. It could be accurate to the last decimal, but is it appropriate to make a judgment solely based on where a company has been? Are we not buying the future–what a company *will* earn? Some figures are on projected earnings. Well, if we only used this number, would that be complete–as if anybody knows what a company will actually earn? Yes, analysts (for the company or independent) can make their best guess, but they often fall short or overstate earnings.

Probably the best gauge would be to take a blend of the "trailing" and the "projected earnings." Many papers report it in some combination: say, trailing 12 and future 12 months. Many use six months back and six months future.

A couple of thoughts:

1. I have been such an adamant proponent of caution in buying stocks. So many investors get caught up in the hype of it all. Yes, I agree we all have to recognize the sensational and buy into it a little–but very little. "Follow earnings, follow earnings," I shout. People who have attended my seminars and even some of my employees have drowned me out. Let me give an example by way of a story.

    Iomega (IOM) is a high-tech software company. The stock reached new highs and kept going up. They announced a stock split (I really like stock splits) and the stock soared. I got in at $14 and $16 and sold out at $30–a really nice profit. The stock went to $50. The hype was still in the air. I bought some $40 options, even though I knew the stock was way overpriced. I got out in days with a double on some and triple on others. The stock went over $60 and headed for $80.

    Everyone was getting in–in both stock and options. I stopped. These numbers put the P/E over 100. I think it hit 120 times earnings at one time.

    At my seminars, in my office, and on W.I.N.™ (our Internet subscription service) I shouted, "I am not playing," "the bubble has got to burst," and "it's way too high." Yes, I might miss out, but this high price can't be sustained. Also, I had been following Iomega for some time as a nice, little, volatile, covered call play, and this time around I wasn't going for it. This all happened between the spring of 1996 and the fall of the same year.

It's hard to buy a stock at $50 when you were buying it for $14 just months before. Yes, it's earnings were up a little, but not that much. The price was not justified.

It did another split. It was a 2:1. The stock split down to the $30 range and went back up to $40. This is when it was at 120 times earnings.

I held no positions, but everyone around me did no matter how hard I tried to stop them. I calculated the stock (based on earnings and a little hype thrown in) ought to be around $23 per share. I was throwing in about $10 per share for the "Internet hype" value. It was really a $12 to $15 stock.

This next part will seem like a joke, but it's true. When the stock was way up there, analysts for the company were trying to justify the high price. They actually made comments like: "The price isn't so high based on projected earnings three years from now." That's right, three years. Talk about hype. But tens of thousands of people bought into it.

Guess what? It fell to $30, then to $24–almost overnight it was at $16. Then it trickled on down to $13. It rebounded to 13^{1}/_{2}$ to 14^{1}/_{2}$ and I started jumping back in. I bought stock, options, and sold puts. I loaded up. I sold out within weeks, before and when it hit $27.

I'll play it a lot, but not when the price is too high. One of the questions you must ask is this: what must the company do to sustain this price? The hypesters that run up a stock are gone; and it could take years to recover from buying too high. Be careful! Follow earnings!

2. The market is crazy, and if not totally wacky, at least hard to understand. This example has played out recently in scenario after scenario. Here's a typical example: a stock is at $60. An analyst (someone with what kind of education? What kind of real-world experience in running companies? What kind of motivation?) projects that in the next year the company will earn $3 per share. He/she calculated this by taking numbers supplied by the company, et cetera, et cetera and putting the

numbers through some kind of filter–possibly what other companies in the same field are saying or doing, and comes up
with the $3. This is a P/E of 20 and not bad for this sector.
He/she recommends the stock as a buy. Not a strong buy, just
a buy, and thousands of investors and funds start to buy. The
stock goes up to $62 on this recommendation, but within weeks
it's back down to $60.

Let's thicken the plot a little with more information. Last year
the company earnings were $2.90 per share. For this type of
business this is a nice profit. The year before it was at $2.40 per
share and the year before that it was $1.50 per share. It's had a
nice increase.

Time passes and the actual earnings are $2.97 per share. The
analyst was off 3¢ and the stock falls to $52, dropping $8 off its
value. You think I'm joking, but I can show you a long list of
this same story played out repeatedly.

The company is profitable, it's growing, it's earning millions–
more than the previous year–but alas, the stock gets killed.
Note: This author looks for these opportunities. See other sec-
tions for taking advantage of these serious dips.

More thoughts on P/E:

1. To make sure you're not overpaying for a stock, watch the P/E
    in changing markets. In a bull market the P/E can be higher. In
    a bear market you would expect a lower P/E.

2. Certain industries have different P/Es. Banks have low P/Es–
    say in the 5 to 12 range. High-tech companies have higher
    P/Es–say around 35 to 60. Check the sector to see what you're
    paying.

3. If your bank P/E is at 15 and the average is 18, you are paying
    a premium for the stock. It's okay if you expect higher earn-
    ings. If your food sector P/E is 16 and the company you're
    considering has a P/E of 12, then you're getting it at a dis-
    count.

4. A low P/E is not a pure indication of value. You need to consider its price volatility (See "Beta"), its range, its direction, and any news you think worthy.

5. You may want to check the historical level (P/E) of the stock. If the current P/E is above the 5 or 15 year historical P/E, the movement of the stock may be about to drop back into line.

Important: The activities or news of a company–that which has driven the P/E to its current level–does you no good prior to your stock purchase. This is why you also need to look at, consider, and take into account the future earnings estimates. Yes, be careful, but remember, you make your money after you buy the stock, so it is the future that will pay you–in dividends and in growth.

YIELDS

A company may take some of the cash it has available and pay it out to the shareholders of record. This is called a dividend. It is done on a per share basis. By dividing the amount of the dividend by the price of each share, you would find the yield or rate of return.

Example: A stock is at $30 and $2 (annual equivalent) is to be paid–that would be a 6.66% return.

Using the dividend yield to determine whether to buy a stock or not is informative, but by no means complete. In the opening sentence I mentioned cash available. I did not say profits or earnings. The dividend could be paid out of debt.

Imagine a company has paid dividends every quarter for 13 years, and every payout is slightly larger than the previous quarter. You think all is well. But lately market share of the company's products are slipping. The directors meet. They've seen their stock value continually rise. They feel the shareholders need to see the dividend and see it in an ever-increasing amount. But their cash flow has dried up. They borrow money for operations and to pay the dividends. They also feel, at first, that they can turn things around.

The dividend is paid like this for five quarters as the company slips toward complete insolvency and possible bankruptcy. Eventually the dividend stops and the stock plummets.

Point: Dividend yield is important but you need to:

1. Keep it in perspective.

2. Seek other information.

   a. Read the company's balance sheets.

   b. Get reports from information sources.

3. Do not rely solely on yields for justification for buying or selling a stock.

GOOD EARNINGS—LOW YIELD

Let's go to the other extreme. A company is doing well. Debt is decreasing, earnings are up and increasing, but the dividend payout is rather small, say 2.1%. What gives? Yes, they can pay out more, but the choice is made not to. Corporate directors in the past 20 years—in our new information society—have had to become experts in many fields. One is taxation.

In the current tax code, dividends are not deductible. The company has to pay taxes on all dividends. The corporation may be in the 15, 25, 31, or 35% tax bracket. When you, the shareholder, receive the dividend, you also have to claim and pay taxes on it—and do so in whatever bracket you are in. This seriously reduces your rate of return. This is double taxation. It's sad that we have politicians who treat us so callously.

Think of this. The company has a $10,000,000 profit. They pay $3,500,000 in taxes. For the sake of this argument, let's say it was all to be paid out in dividends. Your check is $2,000 and you are in the 31% tax bracket. That's an additional $620 to go to the IRS. Yes, the IRS gets 66% in this example. It's a staggering amount. I'd like to comment on the ghastly things they do with this huge amount of money, but I'll restrain myself.

Now imagine a meeting of the directors. If they pay out the money (hopefully from true earnings) to you, they know you will be taxed. The corporation will get taxed no matter what, but they can stop the second level of taxation by simply not paying it. Also, if they could take this money and expand the business, pay down debt—in other words increase the value of the company—would you not be better off?

Remember our earnings multipliers. Let's say the company has a P/E of 15 but it takes this money, using it wisely, and generates 30% more profits. The earnings go way up. Will not the stock value increase? And think, until we sell the stock and have capital gains taxes to pay, the growth is tax free. We could own stock for years with no tax consequences.

Simply put, we want the directors to do the best job they can. If we are investing solely for income (and will take the growth as a bonus) then we may want to find stocks with nice dividend payouts. But most of us should look for companies with great earnings and hope this money is used effectively to build more value into the stocks we own.

BOOK VALUE

When purchasing stock, one has to ask the question, "What is it really worth?" In the real estate arena the cliche answer is, "Whatever someone is willing to pay for it."

It is not quite that simple in picking stocks. One measurement of equity is called the book value. It is the dollar amount you get when you subtract all the liabilities (including preferred stock) from the assets. This figure then could be divided by the number of shares outstanding and get the value per share. With this number in hand, we can see 1) how much of each share is real value–possibly expressed as breakup value; 2) how the book value of the company compares with other companies; and subsequently 3) this value can be used to figure other percentages–as in sales to book–an assessment to determine the percentage of sales to the book value of the company.

Again, the main reason we study this is to make sure we are not overpaying for the stock. I am willing to buy into the excitement of a stock, but when the price gets outrageous, even above that which is justified by earnings and way over book value, then it becomes a little scary.

In theory, you would want what the stock is trading at to be the same as the book value. The book value is $30 per share and the stock is $30 per share. But in reality, many stocks trade at a premium (the share price is above the book value/per share amount) and others trade at a discount (the share price is below the book value per share amount).

Most stocks trade at a premium. I'm constantly on the lookout for companies trading below book value. All else being equal, you're getting the stock wholesale. I really frown on stocks at over three times book value. If the earnings justify the higher price, I might go for it. But I like stock trading at one and a half to two times the book value. If you are after stocks that trade even, you'll have to look a long time and possibly end up buying nothing.

Don't despair when you see a great company at two and a half to three and a half times book value. Consider the following: a company has purchased real estate–buildings and factories. They also own a lot of equipment. These are all depreciable items for tax purposes.

According to GAAP (Generally Accepted Accounting Principles) a company must carry on its books the value of these assets at *cost* or *market,* whichever is *less.* This adds an unrealistic dimension to the calculation of book value.

An example is in order. XYZ Company purchases a $10,000,000 factory. It depreciates it over the years to $6,000,000, but in fact the building is actually worth $14,000,000. The amount on the company books (as an asset) is $6,000,000. The same with trucks, computers, and other equipment. And these depreciate faster. You see by this how difficult it is to get a proper "fix" on what a company is really worth.

To protect yourself:

1. Go out and "kick the tires"–really check the company out. Do your homework.

2. Learn how to get "behind the scenes" financial information.

3. Use book value in conjunction with other measuring devices.

Not all low book value companies are bad deals. Usually a low book value means there is not a large belief that a stock price will increase. Maybe it's in an unfavorable industry. There are many good companies with low book values. Also, there are companies ready to explode which have a current high book value ratio.

One possible play is to look for companies with low book value because they are often the target of a takeover. Other companies want to get at their assets and can buy at bargain rates if the stock is trading at or below book value, or if the book value figure does not properly represent true book value.

Book value is extremely important. Look for companies with a low book value percentage, but keep everything in perspective. Book value is also referred to as "Shareholder Equity." What kind of income and growth do you want your equity to produce?

EQUITY RETURNS

I hinted at this in the last section on book value. We want our equity to be producing for us. In real estate, it's how much income it can produce. Department stores measure part of their success by "sales per square foot." What are our assets making?

Return on stock equity is the company's after tax profits divided by the book value. The important thing here is to see if this return is increasing from year to year. These numbers are usually found in the company's annual report.

DEBT RATIO

I've saved the best till last. Actually, this is not the most important measurement of stock value–that realm is reserved for earnings, but this runs a close second place.

This ratio shows the percentage of debt a company has in relationship to shareholder equity. You want debt ratio to be low. The actual figure varies from company to company. Just remember debt is a killer of businesses. Yes, the company may have a well-marketed product; yes, cash flow is up, but it may not be enough to cover the debt load.

Let's say a company has shareholder equity of $100,000,000. Debt is $30,000,000. This is a ratio of 30%. Some companies have debt as high as 70 to 90%. That is way too high, because the earnings are decreased so much to service the debt.

This author (again, many other variables enter the picture) wants the debt to be under 30%. I usually shy away from 50% or higher debt ratios.

There are several other smaller measurement techniques, and all are helpful to a certain extent. The "Big 5" just mentioned should be in your toolbox to help you make intelligent and timely decisions.

No one measurement alone is foolproof, and even when all five point to a recommended buy, the whole market may turn down.

Remember that these tools are to help you take the best-calculated risk possible. When in doubt, remember my strongest advice from my seminars: "Follow earnings."

6

OPTIMUM OPTIONS

More bang for the buck! That's what we all want. Wise use of stock options is one way to get it. This chapter is about using a form of proxy investing to leverage greater returns. And returns, to me, mean extra income, not just an increase in value.

Throughout all my real estate books and courses and now in my stock market educational materials, I stress "cash flow" concepts and techniques. After all, is it not cash flow that pays the bills and lets us get into an ever-increasing upward spiral of income?

Buying or selling options to purchase stock are simple strategies loaded with opportunities. There are variations on purchase and exit strategies, and combination plays both with the underlying stock and with other options. Options are derivatives of an investment on an underlying security. A call option is the right to buy a stock at a fixed strike price anytime before a set date. A put option is similar, but is the right to sell. Both calls and puts expire. They end. This expiration is one inherent risk of option investing.

Why would anyone want such a risk? Simply because of the fantastic profits which can be made in a very short period of time. You see, an option moves up and down in value with the movement of the stock, but to be precise, it moves on an exaggerated scale. I'll explain this as I go along and illustrate it with examples. Once we're through with the basics (and I refer you to the books, *Wall Street Money Machine, Volumes 1* and *4* for more details) I'll show you a few heavy-duty strategies to get you making more money.

Example: you could buy a stock for $86. The stock seems down right now; you think it will go back up to $92 or $96, where it's been trading for some time. It's March. You check the April $90 call options (the right to buy the stock at $90 per share before the April expiration date). The call options are $2.50 each. You'll spend $250 plus commission for one contract (a contract contains 100 shares of stock). $2,500 would purchase 10 contracts. You could also buy the $85 calls, the $95 calls, or other strike prices, and you might be better served by buying options with a different expiration month than April. (I explore short-term and long-term plays in other special reports and in other chapters.)

Your $2.50 option premium gives you the right to buy the stock at $90. Obviously you want the stock to rise. Many people suggest the stock would have to go to $92.50 for you to break even and above that for any profit. A better understanding of the strategy, though, will help you see that the stock doesn't have to rise that high for us to be profitable.

Options are bought and sold like stocks. There is a trader (like a market maker or specialist) who buys and sells. Like stock, you don't know who purchases your option–it just happens. Options have bids and asks. A bid is what you can sell it for, the ask is the price you pay to buy. The bid and the ask move up and down according to several factors: 1) the supply and demand for the option, 2) the time left before the expiration date, and 3) other market sentiments. For example, with tremendously erratic stock, the market makers keep a high option premium because they know the stock has the potential to make big swings. Also note that you do not have to trade at the current bid and ask. You can place orders to buy below the ask or an order to sell above the bid. These orders can be day orders only or "Good Till Canceled" (GTC) orders. It costs nothing to place the order.

STOCK/STRIKE	STOCK PRICE	OPTION (CALL)
	$84	$1.00
XYZ Company	85	2.00
April $90 Call option	86	2.50
	87	3.00
	88	3.75
Note: The premium depends on	90	4.75
time before expiration.	91	5.50
	92	6.50

Watch the movement of the option compared with the stock price in the example. Look at the $88 price. The option is $3.75. This will not stay constant. This $88/$3.75 quote is, say, six weeks before the expiration date. If it were six days, the option could be $1.25. You see, an option buys time. A part of the premium is the time value. In our example, the $3.75 is all time value. Why did it go down to $1.25? Because "the invisible market" doesn't believe very strongly that in six days the stock will go up to or above $90. If the stock stays at $88, the option will probably expire worthless. However, look at what happens when the stock goes above $90. The option has become more valuable. Someone is willing to pay $4.75 for the right to buy the stock at $90. If the stock goes to $98, the option could be worth $8 to $9 (or more), again depending on the time left before expiration.

If the stock is $92 and the option is $6.50, you see that $2 of the $6.50 is actually paying for stock. The option is "in the money" by $2 (intrinsic value). The remaining $4.50 of the option premium is time value (extrinsic value).

Now, the main question: what is our purpose in buying the option? Do we want to buy the stock? Maybe, but this author is waiting for the options to gain value so they can be sold at a profit. If we purchased the options for $2.50 and can now sell it for $4.50 (assuming the bid and ask is something like $4.50 x $4.75), we have a $2 profit. If we had purchased ten contracts, that would be $2,000.

Let's review the word "exaggerated." In this example a $1 movement in the stock means a 50¢ movement in the option. Sometimes the stock to option movement ratio could be "tick for tick," or dollar for dollar. A dollar rise in the stock produces a dollar rise in the option.

The point is you have much less cash tied up–$2,500 controls 1,000 shares of stock. You didn't invest $86,000 buying 1,000 shares of stock. Also, a $1 move in the stock from $86 to $87 is around a 1% gain. If this creates a 50¢ move in the option from $2.50 to $3, it is a 20% gain.

If you sell the $2.50 option for $4.50, the $4,500 cash will be in your account tomorrow. Options clear in one day.

After attending the first day of your workshop, I was confident that with some diligence one could in fact use the techniques you taught. The second day in class, with increased confidence, I made my first two rolling option purchases during the morning's "early bird" session.

To my pleasant surprise, I was able to sell both options the following morning for a profit large enough to cover the complete cost of the workshop. I have contributed around $31,125 in the last 15 days, and thus have been able to clear a net profit of $23,252.35 after commissions. Yes, that's right, 74.7% in 15 days and an annual percentage rate of 1,817%.

I'm still pinching myself to see if I'm awake! I am now eagerly waiting to attend The Next Step™ workshop and hold even greater expectations in mind.

—MICHAEL, WA

Yes, we've all seen stock go up $2 to $10 in, or within, a day. Think about buying an option an hour after the market opens for 50¢ and selling it for $1.50 two hours later. Ten contracts would generate a $1,000 profit.

Let's do the same on a put. A few years ago, Fannie Mae (FNM) did a 4:1 stock split. A few months later, the stock was rolling between $31.50 and $36. News came out that the long bond yield was down three points. This is the U.S. Treasury 30-year bond. The stock market was hammered that day. There were other things going on also. Fannie Mae is very interest-rate sensitive, as they borrow money at one rate and lend it out at another, higher rate. If the interest rates go up (that's why the long bond was falling–fear of inflation and a rise in rates), the stock can really go down. Likewise, if interest rates go down, the stock might go up.

To put it mildly, the stock got slammed. I knew it would go down. I put it on the Wealth Information Network™ (W.I.N.™) immediately, telling my students how I was going to play it. The stock closed Friday at about $33. It opened at $31.75 (on a 30-minute delayed opening). I purchased the March $32.50 puts.

This lets me "put" the stock to someone else at $32.50. If the stock goes under $32.50, my put option becomes more valuable. It's the opposite of a call. As the stock goes down, the put becomes worth more. I bought these puts for $1^1/8 or $1.125. The stock went down to $27^1/2 and as it bounced back up to $29 to $30, I sold the put for $3^5/8. That's a four-hour play and a nice profit of $2,500. $3,625 minus $1,125 = $2,500 (minus commissions of about $110 for both trades).

If you buy options, you do not have the obligation to buy or sell the stock. You also don't have to sell the option—you could just let it expire. You have the "right" to buy or sell. Again, though, I don't buy the options to buy the stock. I buy options hoping for an increase in value and then sell them. It's just quick-turn money.

I have a "bear market mentality" in the midst of a bull market. I really don't like losing money. Options are very risky—only 15 to 20% of contracts ever get exercised. That's not to say there are many losses, as some investors like me get in and get out rapidly. I have lost on several plays, and each time I do, I vow to never do that again. I want to learn from my mistakes; I've cut the losses to a bare minimum. You can watch me do option trades on W.I.N.™, Stock Market Institute of Learning's subscription Internet service.

Here is how my trades have gone since I started using W.I.N.™ I bought two Xerox (XRX) $125 April call options for $6.75 and sold them one week later for $10.75, a profit of $663 (49.1%). I also bought two Warner Lambert (WLA) $90 April call options for $6.75 and just sold them nine days later for $10.25, a profit of $562 (41.6%).

I'm shooting for 50% returns on covered call writing, all prof-its to be reinvested until I'm consistently pulling enough per month to be able to retire and do what I want with my life. Now there's hope and light at the end of the tunnel. All my thanks go to Wade and everybody there on the W.I.N.™ staff.

—AUGUSTIN

You'll see my "hunker down," try-not-to-lose-a-penny strategies permeating the following formulas.

BUY ON DIPS

One of my longtime favorite ways to make money on options is to buy when the stock takes a serious dip. Check the company's story though, to avoid further downturns. Look at the following charts:

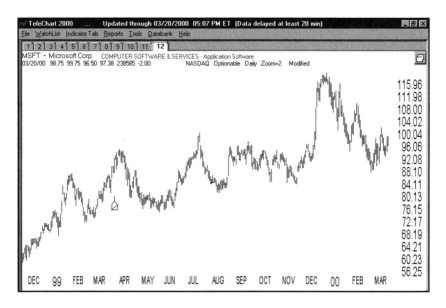

MICROSOFT (MSFT)
The stock rolled between $90 and $98 during late 1999. When the stock got down to $90, I purchased $90 and $95 calls. When the stock rose, I sold the calls at a nice profit. I'm always doing this play with a dozen or so companies.

TeleChart 2000 ... Updated through 03/20/2000 05:07 PM ET (Data delayed at least 20 min)
File WatchList IndicatorTab Reports Tools Databank Help
RNBO - Rainbow Technologies Inc   COMPUTER SOFTWARE & SERVICES - Security Software & Services
03/20/00 41.25 41.88 39.25 39.63 1020 -2.37   NASDAQ Optionable Daily Zoom=2 Modified

RAINBOW TECHNOLOGIES (RNBO)
I like Rainbow Technologies (RNBO). When it dipped down to $37, I jumped back in it. I'm doing it as a covered call play. There are so many companies that fall into this category.

ROLLING OPTIONS

After a company takes a big dip, the climb back up is volatile. Sometimes it stays down for a while and starts trading between a certain range. I call this rolling stock. If you follow my formula for a pure rolling stock play as outlined in the *Wall Street Money Machine, Volume 1* and at our live Wall Street Workshop™, you'll realize that $50 to $100 stocks don't fit the basic formula. They're priced too high. Your cash goes a short distance with an $80 stock. $8,000 buys 100 shares. Yes, a move to $85 would make you $500, but a $5 move on a $5 stock would also make you $500, but with only $500 tied up. A better example: $8,000 would purchase 1,600 shares of a $5 stock. A $5 move up would double your money. Upon selling you'd have $16,000–a profit of $8,000. Now to make it more exciting and still double your money (because there are many more companies at $80 which can easily go to $85 than there are companies at $5 which go to $10), let's play an option.

The stock is at $80. You call your broker and buy the $85 call options, say two months out. You pay $2.25 per option and buy 10 contracts for $2,250. The stock moves up to $84. Your option is worth

$4.75. You sell for a $2.50 profit and make $2,500. Look at the power of leverage.

Options allow you to invest in the big stocks by proxy, using a small amount of money.

Look at the chart on Microsoft. Many times as the stock goes down to $100 to $102, I buy the $100 or $105 call option. I'm not hoping the stock goes back up to $120, though it would be nice, and I'm not doing this to buy the stock. I'm simply going to sell my $2.25 option for $3.50 or $4 when the stock rolls up. Another day, another week, another $10,000 profit.

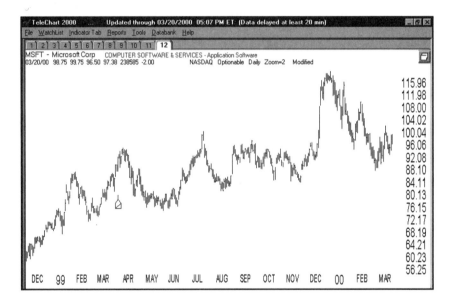

Some stocks just seem to trade in a certain range (support at the bottom, resistance at the top.) Check out Bear Sterns (BSC). It rolls between $37 and $42. When it gets down to $37 or $39, I buy the $35 calls or the $40 calls if they are cheap. I sell them when the stock gets to $40 to $42. Don't get greedy. Get out and get your profits working better somewhere else.

Wade Cook's workshop . . . was a skeptical seminar for me to go to, even though I have invested in the stock market for several years. My first attempt at options was at the Wall Street Work-

shop™ last week. I generated $3,256 in one day's time while at the workshop! Since then, in the next week, I made another $2,270. I am excited about the opportunity to be home with my children while I am making money for my husband's and my retirement. Thank you for teaching me a few formulas and hands-on experience.

—Dawn, CA

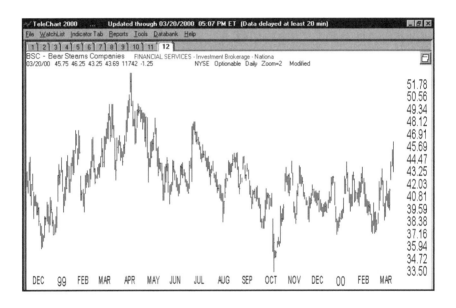

Selling Straddles

By definition, a straddle is buying a call option and a put option on the same stock with the same strike price and expiration date. In the sameness is the simplicity. The same stock. The same number of contracts (call and put). The same strike price, if it's a pure straddle. You could also buy an $80 put and a $90 call on an $85 stock with the same expiration date. Notice that I am buying both a call and a put. This gives me two plays on the volatility, or movement. Though it is not exactly doubling my potential, it does come close to doing that.

There are some potentially expensive risks, however. This is not a strategy for everyone. If the stock suddenly makes a big move in either direction, I make a lot of money. Remember, I haven't bought any stock and I have the right to sell the stock to, or buy stock from, someone.

If the stock goes up I sell the call for a profit. I still own the put. If the stock subsequently takes a dip, I can sell the put at break-even, a slight loss, or at a profit on a big dip.

Before I write a straddle, I spend a lot of time with my broker evaluating what the profits and risk of loss could be. I won't typically do a straddle unless the reward potential and the cash flow are substantial, and the risk is low. You'll need to make your own decisions in this area. This strategy has worked lately because of the extremely volatile stocks in the high-tech sector.

HEDGE A STOCK

One last use for options is a "hedge." A hedge is like an insurance policy. You hedge to limit your downside.

Let's say you just spent $10,000 and purchased 100 shares of stock at $100 each. You think the stock is low (either the company is really profitable or that the stock has gone down–hit a low). That's a lot of money to have tied up. You have unlimited upside potential and all the time in the world because you actually own the stock. Your only risk is a dip in the price of the stock.

To ensure against a loss in your stock value, buy a $100 put, or even a $95 put (if you are willing to lose a little). Yes, you could put in a stop loss, at, say, $97 and only lose $300, but what about a drop to $70 wherein you could lose $3,000. The $100 put is, say, $2. One contract (controlling 100 shares–the same amount you own) would cost $200 plus commission. If you never exercise the put, that's $200 out the window. You bought the stock hoping it would go up, and if it does your $200 ($2 put) goes down in value. Any increase in the value of your $10,000 investment will be offset by this loss. However, if the stock goes down, and I mean seriously down, this $200 will be money well spent. If the stock goes down to $80 (assuming this is still before the expiration date of the put) your put will be worth at least $20. It could be $22 to $25 depending on any time value still built into the put premium.

Think of this: You could sell the stock for $80 and also sell the put premium for $20. That's $8,000 and $2,000 respectively. You've broken even. You see the insurance-against-loss aspect of this. You could lose $200 or at least have your profits offset by this amount, but you can make up all your losses with the proper put.

Two more ideas: The $95 put might be purchased for 25¢ when the stock is at $100. One contract would be $25 plus commissions. This lower strike price and the corresponding lower put premium will let you buy a put further out (say five to six months) for a lower price. Your risk is $500 plus the put premium. Why $500? Because you've lost the amount between $100 for the stock and $95 for the option. One hundred shares times $5 equals $500.

The $100 put is $2 and it's only out one to two months. I usually buy the short-term puts at the higher strike price (out one to two months and then reevaluate the situation: company news, the stock price near the expiration date, et cetera) or further out puts below the strike price. They're cheaper but also give you more time.

By looking at the company's chart you can determine how much you want to spend, how much time you want to buy, and how much risk you want to hedge.

COMBO

You could also buy a call with a $100 or $110 strike price. If you're certain this stock is a winner, go ahead and buy the stock for $10,000, but spend $500 and purchase the $105 calls out two to three months. If the stock rises, you'll see first hand how the riskier option plays produce the greater returns.

7

THE PUT-TING GREEN

This chapter was written to dispel the mystery of "put" options and give several serious strategies for generating cash flow from either buying or selling puts.

A put option, as opposed to a call option, gives an investor the right to sell a stock. We will be concerned with stock options only in this chapter. A put option could be defined in street jargon as the right to "put it to someone." You would want to put a stock to someone when you can purchase the stock at a lower price and sell it (immediately) at a higher price. For example, if you notice a stock consistently climbing above $30 to $33 or $35, and it not only has a hard time getting to the higher level, but also has a hard time sustaining the higher price, then you may want to buy a $35 put. As the stock comes back down, your "right" to sell the stock for $35 increases in value. As with call options, I do not buy the option to sell the stock. I buy the option to sell the option.

MORE ABOUT SELLING OPTIONS

Options are fickle. They don't always mirror the exact stock movement. A lot of things enter the picture:

1. The volatility of the stock. What does the options market know? Sometimes, it seems they know more than the stock market.

2. The time remaining before the option expires. After all, when buying an option you are paying for two things: time (extrinsic value), and part of the price of the stock (intrinsic value) if you are purchasing an "in the money" option.

If you purchase a $2 call option on a $35 strike price when the stock is at $33, and the stock moves to $36, your option could easily be worth $4 to $6, depending on the time left before the expiration date. However, if the stock goes nowhere, and then rises to $36 with ten days to go before the expiration date, it may only be worth the same $2. If the stock halts at $36 and the time elapses to the point that there is only a day or so left, the option may trade for just the one dollar that the option is in the money. In this example, a $36 stock with a $35 strike price is $1 in the money. When investing in options, time is both our friend and our enemy. The value of the option has a direct and distinct relationship to the expiration date. All other factors–price, volatile movement, and market maker maneuvering–aid and abet the "fixed time" aspect of the option value. Hence, options can be extremely profitable, yet very risky.

Stock options are sold in 100 share increments. When you purchase one contract, you are actually purchasing the right to buy or sell 100 shares. Strike prices are the same for calls and puts. Stocks priced in the $5 to $25 range are sold in $2.50 increments. Stocks priced in the $25 to $200 range are sold in $5 increments, and stocks priced above $200 are sold in $10 increments. Note: as the options market becomes more popular, there are more strike prices added. For example, if a stock has a high trading volume, the option "market maker" may add an additional strike price, such as $32.50 or $57.50. Also, stocks splits cause odd strike prices.

THE "PUT" OPTION

Stock options are different from other options in that you actually control the right to buy or sell the underlying security.

Let's keep exploring the "put" option. Keep in mind, if you are following the Wade Cook formula, you are not purchasing the option to purchase the stock, but to have inventory to sell as the option increases in value. Look at the following chart and you'll see an increasing put value.

STOCK	STRIKE	PUT OPTION
$34	$35	$2.00
33	35	2.50
32	35	3.25
31	35	4.50
30	35	5.75
29	35	7.00
28	35	8.00

Example: It's October and we purchased the January $35 puts.

Your put option increases in value as the stock moves down and away from the strike price. If the stock is $31 and the strike price is $35, the value of your option has to be at least $4. Indeed, you could buy the stock at $31 and sell it to someone for $35. This put option gives you that right.

Options expire on the third Friday of the month, but you may exercise your option at any time on or before the expiration date. Or, you may sell your option anytime there is an open bid. Options have a bid and an ask like stocks. You can sell at any price you choose, and one of those choices may be a market order (which is also known as the current bid).

The sentence that brings options to life and the one I repeat in all my seminars holds true for put options as well. Here it is:

When there is a small movement in the stock, there is a magnified movement in the option.

Revisit the previous diagram. A move of $3 in stock price, about 10% down in the stock, took the option from $2.50 to $4.50, a huge percentage move. With a call option you don't need to double the price of the stock to double your money on the option, and with put options you don't need a stock to drop half of its value to double your put option value. Frequently, small stock movements equal large option movements.

When the options start moving, you have several choices.

1. Sell it for a price you're happy with.

    a. This could be done by placing a sell order anytime after you own the option, even immediately—usually at a higher price.

    b. You can wait and watch the stocks, trying to plan your exit to maximize your profits.

Which one do you choose? In my case it usually depends on how busy I am. If I have a lot of plays going on, or if my other business endeavors take up my time, I usually place the sell order when I make my purchase. I place it high enough to get a nice large profit. If the option doesn't move that high, I move the price down or just go ahead and sell. Note: pay special attention as the expiration date nears.

2. Exercise the underlying stock (buy or sell), but again, this is not why I play options.

3. Sell part of your position, five contracts out of the ten. Ride the five you keep to greater profits. It's possible to get a free ride, in that the profits from the five contracts you sold could "get back" all or most of your investment. Now, you have nothing to lose.

Before I get into specific strategies, let me remind you of the underlying current of my trades—it is to make millions by executing minor trades, even on the same stock, at different strike prices and expiration months. Why?

1. I don't have a lot of cash tied up in any one deal.

2. I can take advantage of frequent, small swings and not wait for rare, "killer" moves.

3. I like the cash flow. There are always other deals. Take all or some of your profits and jump back in if the stock moves back

up, choosing a different strike price. If you sold your $35 strike price and more bad news came out, maybe a purchase of the $30 strike price would be in order. If the stock has dipped way down and you're highly profitable, take some of your money and:

a. Buy some of the stock–hoping for a rebound.

b. Buy call options and ride the stock back up.

c. Generate more cash flow by selling puts (see the section on selling puts), or do bull put spreads.

There are three put formulas that you can use for generating income. I hope you'll note that inherent to these formulas are the "risk eliminators," which, hopefully, will keep us out of trouble.

FORMULA #1–ROLLING OPTIONS

The development of this formula has its genesis in my rolling stock strategy. Play options on stocks trading within a specific range. I like the less expensive stocks because it doesn't take too much movement to make a great profit. However, most stocks that are doing nice, steady rolls between a high and a low are in higher dollar amounts, say between $98 and $104. It would take a lot of cash to buy them, and there just may be a better use of our money. If the roll continues, there is definitely a better way to play the roll: proxy investing. Do options on stocks that trade within a certain range.

The strategy is simple: buy call options when the stock is low and wait for the roll up. Next, sell the call option and then buy put options when the stock peaks. Take your profits when it rolls back down. I've written about this concept elsewhere so I won't belabor the call play here. Let's explore the put strategy.

Volatility, predictability, and using the extra cash which you can afford to lose, brings a higher degree of certainty to this risky arena. This is a tremendous formula in which you can get to be an expert.

FORMULA #2–PUT VARIATIONS

This formula requires volatility, but we also like predictability. I'll encourage you once again to subscribe to a charting service. (I use Telechart 2000® by Worden Brothers. Stock Market Institute of Learning™ has some really great video seminar productions on charting. Call 1-800-872-7411.)

To begin, you track a stock. Let's say it continues to peak (hits resistance) every time it gets to $35. Obviously it could break out at any point and go to a new high, so make sure you can stand the risk, but for the past while it hasn't gone above $35.

STOCK PRICE	$30 PUT	$35 PUT	$40 PUT
34.75	1.50	3.00	6.75
34.00	1.25	3.38	7.25
33.00	1.75	4.00	8.125
32.00	2.50	4.75	9.00
30.00	4.00	6.50	10.50
28.00	6.00	7.875	12.50
27.00	6.75	8.75	13.50

For quite a few months $35 has been the high. Buy the $35 put, or if you think the stock is going to go way down, play the $30 put. Let's say the stock is at $34³/4. The $35 put is $3. That's a fairly high premium. Very little of the option premium is in the money with this put. "In the money" means the stock is below the strike price. In this case, just 25¢ is in the money. We check the $30 puts and they're going for 75¢. They're cheap because the stock, at this strike price, is so far out of the money. The stock has to take a big move downward for you to get to the $30 strike price. Now remember, the stock doesn't have to get to $30 to make money on the option. Depending on the time left to expiration, your option could double to $1.50, then go to $2.50 on a one or two dollar down-tick in the stock. You can sell at a profit anytime, and you can sell the option anytime before it expires.

Now check the $40 put. (To check if one exists, see if a bid and an ask are being written.) It might be going for $6¹/2 x $6³/4 bid and ask. Think of this: the stock is at $34³/4. It's $5.25 in the money ($40 strike price minus $34.75 = $5.25). Part of your put option premium is intrinsic value ($5.25). The balance is time value. You're paying $1.50 ($6.75 - $5.25 = $1.50) for time. This is also referred to as extrinsic value. It's what you're paying for the time needed for this stock to do something.

This strike price is so far in the money that the relationship between the stock movement and the option movement may be in close ratio. (See Delta Formula in the *Wall Street Money Machine, Volume 1.*) The stock goes to $33 and your $6.75 option goes to $8. (A $1.75 downward movement in the stock increases your option value of $1.25 up to $8.) Now the stock goes to $30 and your option is worth $11. A nice relationship—a nice profit. Sell it for a nice gain. Even if the stock continues down you have a nice profit. (If you still think it hasn't hit bottom and you still have time before the expiration date, you may want to wait and try to get $12 or $13.) You'll kick yourself if the stock starts back up. As the stock price rises, the value of your $11 put option decreases.

Take the profit and use some of it to buy a $30 or $35 call option, or get in on a different play.

1. Options are a fixed time investment.

2. You should be doing this with money you can afford to lose.

3. You should choose a month far enough out for the stock to perform as you hope.

I really like in-the-money options, but not too far in the money. The $40 put in the last example looked nice, but to double our money we need a large movement in the stock. $6.75 to $12 or $13 requires a stock at $27 or $28.

STOCK PRICE	$30 PUT	$35 PUT	$40 PUT
34.75	1.50	3.00	6.75
34.00	1.25	3.38	7.25
33.00	1.75	4.00	8.125
32.00	2.50	4.75	9.00
30.00	4.00	6.50	10.50
28.00	6.00	7.875	12.50
27.00	6.75	8.75	13.50

No, I don't have to double my money on the option to be happy–
a 20 to 40% profit in a few days is just fine–but it is a calculation I make
in my head. Some stockbrokers have a computer model which gives a
"% to double" to see how much of a movement is needed in the time
available.

The $35 put and the $30 put require much smaller movements to
be profitable. Look at the previous diagram to see a comparison.

Look at the tremendous leverage in the $30 put. Obviously you
can lose if the stock doesn't move way down, and obviously there's
some safety in the $40 put–because it's so far in the money, but you
get your greatest bang for the buck on the cheaper options.

Also note that in rare cases there may be $32.50 puts and $37.50
puts. You could check and see.

Next point: You should check the option price for several different
expiration dates. Look at your charts and make sure you give the stock/
option plenty of time to move. If it goes through adverse swings, you
still have time to recover.

What if the value of your option goes down? You have three choices:

1. Wait it out (perhaps get in your order to sell at a price you like,
    so you don't have to check on it every day).

2. Sell it at a loss and lose all or some of your money.

3. Buy more at the lower price. Jump back in if you still like the
    story.

EXAMPLES

*Dell (DELL): Rolls between $35 and $50. At the time this chapter was written it had just
moved up to $57. Maybe it will go up more, or maybe it will establish a new roll range or
climb to an all time high.*

General Motors (GM): This rolls between $73 and $83.

*Microsoft (MSFT): This is so often in the news that it's a natural. When this chapter was
written it was rolling between $90 and $100. This has been a great cash flow machine. I wish
it would never quit–except for perhaps a new stock split just seconds after it dips and I've
loaded up on call options–well, I can have dreams, too.*

Update: This is odd. MSFT has done two 2:1 stock splits since this book was first published as *Stock Market Miracles.* Now, as *Volume 2* of the *Wall Street Money Machine Series* I was readying this section for the new revised edition. Amazingly, I didn't have to change the last paragraph at all. Also, MSFT hopefully is nearing a court settlement with the meddling Feds so the stock is very news driven.

FORMULA #3—PEAK PROFITS

Buying put options when a stock has had a tremendous run up will have the same timing, and the same in-the-money, and out-of-the-money pricing as a rolling option which has peaked. However, there is one substantial difference and this difference can make you a lot of money—very quickly.

Here is how it works. Every day there are several stocks that close several dollars higher. They usually move higher on news. Sometimes, but very seldom, they do so for no reason whatsoever. The good news is usually about earnings—and if the earnings are great, the new high might be sustained, but if it's something other than earnings, i.e. a takeover, a merger, new product, stock split, et cetera, the news can play out very quickly.

As in the "Dead Cat Bounce" strategy, the Peak strategy happens very quickly. You have to be ready to move—not only on the purchase, but also to sell. I usually know my exit (sell price) when I get involved.

There are so many examples it is difficult to only choose three or four for this chapter. There are sometimes hundreds a day. I go for the big moves, so let's show you how to do this, right after we explain the play.

A stock goes up $8 in one day—on whatever news. It goes from $52 to $60 between 2:30 P.M. and closing at 4:00 P.M. (Eastern Time). It stops right around $60. We wait. There may be additional good or bad news after the market closes. If you think it has peaked, buying it now might be the move.

The next morning we check the news; we see the direction of the stock—waiting for resistance, or a good top. Usually this means the stock starts moving back down. This top may take several days to establish. The $8 run up was great, but it goes up $2 the next day and then about noon on the third day, after it's gone up another dollar, it gives back that $1 and even drops another 50¢.

If you think the news has played out, consider buying the $60 put or the $65 put. Let's say the $65 put is going for $6 (the stock is at $62.50) while the $60 put is $4. Then over the next several weeks or months the stock gives back one-half of the $10 plus run-up. Your put value will grow drastically.

I usually buy these out a month or two. If I do them short term—two weeks to six weeks–I usually do in-the-money options ($65 put). If I play out further and there is no new news on the horizon (earnings reports won't be out for another two months, et cetera), I'll play out-of-the-money puts–say $60 or even the $55 put if I'm feeling wild.

3 Com (COMS)

3 Coms (COMS) moved up in early 2000 on anticipation of its upcoming IPO/spinoff of Palm (PALM), going as high as $119. When the IPO came out in early March, the stock moved back down in a hurry.

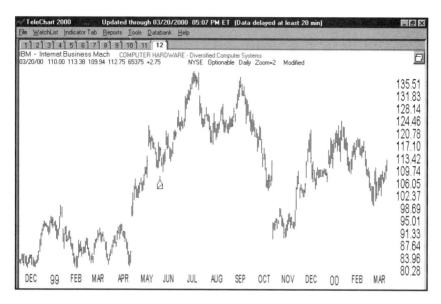

INTERNATIONAL BUSINESS MACHINES (IBM)
International Business Machines (IBM) announced a 2:1 stock split.

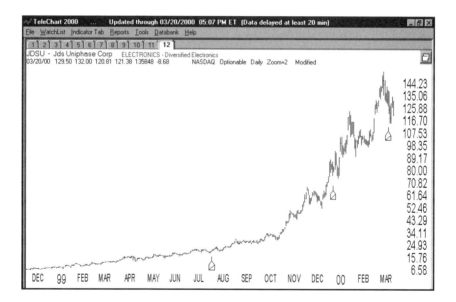

JDS UNIPHASE (JDS)
JDS Uniphase (JDS) announced a stock split and then within days of the actual split, announced another stock split.

The list is endless. I believe we live in a very short-term society. We forget good news in about three days. It takes three months to forget bad news. This is only my conjecture, "the gospel according to Wade." I have no empirical evidence to back up the three-day/three-month statement, only a string of trades used as a guideline.

EXAMPLES

Yes, you can make money on both up and down stock movements. Use these strategies for maximum cash flow.

Cisco (CSCO)
Cisco (CSCO) shows a lot of volatility and the ups and downs create many opportunities to play calls and puts.

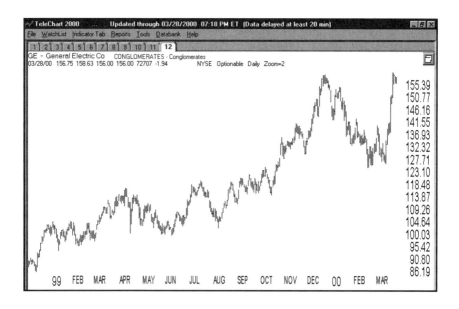

GENERAL ELECTRIC (GE)

General Electric (GE) announcved a 3:1 split in February 2000. Since the split date isn't until June, the stock trended down.

Note: Just because a stock splits doesn't mean it immediately starts climbing up. Sometimes there's a sell off (or whatever) and the stock goes down. See how to play these movements under Stock Splits.

DIFFERENT PEAK PLAYS

1. Earnings news. Many company stocks have a 5 to 10% jump on good earnings news. Be careful, however. Sometimes earnings are up but the stock goes down. This usually occurs when the earnings are not as good as some analysts projected. This news plays out really fast. Many people buy the stock in hopes of a better dividend. The short run up is truly short. The stock doesn't always go back down to where it was before the last bit of news, but many times I've seen it go lower. I think the reason for this is that the stock was already up in anticipation of good news (company leaks, press speculation, et cetera). There usually is no long-term stability for the "jumped up" higher price. Rather, the direction is down. This is one of my favorite formulas. Why? Because we make money so fast.

2. Mergers and acquisitions–especially failed attempts when companies take over other companies. I usually like to play the one being taken over. If the attempt fails, or takes longer than expected, the stocks go down–witness Chrysler (C) a while ago. There are two plays:

   a. If there is a lot of debt involved (especially acquisition of new debt), as compared to a stock swap, the bigger company's (the one doing the takeover or merger) stock may see a quick–usually small–run up and then come down as investor euphoria cools. Sometimes the terms of the deal have a chilling effect.

   b. The baby company's stock may run up to the take over price, but quickly cool with the lapse of time. This may be time for call options (not put options) if the takeover is friendly and the price is right.

3. Spin-offs: When a big company spins off a division or subsidiary and a lot of cash is to be generated, there is usually a nice up tick in the stock. From my experience, though, it is short-lived. Why? The company selling off usually has other problems (the core business is in trouble) and the directors are pressured by shareholder groups to liquidate assets to get the main business going or to distribute cash dividends, et cetera. The problems don't go away easily and the stock dribbles back down.

4. Stock splits: Stock splits offer so many opportunities, I cannot do justice to them here. I've written extensively on them in the *Wall Street Money Machine, Volume 1* and *Volume 4* and I do many plays (with explanations) on our subscription internet service (W.I.N.™ = Call 1-800-872-7411 for details or check out W.I.N.™ at www.wadecook.com). We'll just deal with the put play in this chapter.

The key is to watch and wait. If the stock runs way up on the announcement of the stock split and continues to climb on other good news announcements like an increase in dividends, just be patient. It will probably take a dip.

Remember:

1. The stock is probably entering new territory–it may be ripe for a sell off as investors take their profits.

2. There are whole market swings, or at least sector swings (sympathy moves?) to contend with.

3. Other news–competition from others, charge offs, et cetera–may affect the stock.

Remember most stocks just don't go up in a straight line. Wait for true strength, check your charts (stochastic, market sentiments, et cetera) and ride the stock down with a put option.

Following are some other charts for your perusal. The point of putting these here is to show volatility.

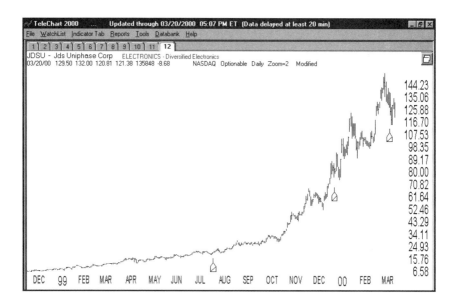

Look what happens after the split. Sometimes they go up and level off, but sometimes they go down.

Wait for weakness.

Sometimes the stock goes nowhere. It may be so high before the split that there is nowhere to go in the short term (usually due to stock-holders selling off to lock in their gains), so the stock falls. These are hard to time. I usually wait for weakness and buy the call before I start playing puts. I want it to establish a roll pattern or run up to a new high. In short: to play puts we need all indicators pointing to a decrease in the stock price.

SELLING PUTS

I've written on this in another chapter entitled "Selling Puts." But in this chapter on puts, it is necessary to mention the gist of the strategy.

Like calls, puts can be bought and sold. Up until now, this chapter has only dealt with buying puts–then selling (closing out a position) on puts we've previously purchased.

Now let's explore selling put options on stocks we don't own. If buying a put gives us the right to put the stock to someone else, then selling this right would allow someone to put the stock to us. We would have an obligation to purchase the stock. (This is the exact opposite of writing a covered call.)

Why would we do this? Two reasons.

1. To generate cash. When we sell a put we get that premium into our account tomorrow.

2. We want to own the stock at a lower price, or at least be willing to buy it at the put strike price.

I love this strategy. An example would be in order. A stock is at $13.50. It's been rolling between $12 and $15, but you think it may break out and go way up.

You sell the October (one or two months out) $15 put for $3.50, or the $12.50 put for $1. One contract would generate $350, the other $100. Ten contracts would get you $3,500, or $1,000.

What have you done? You've agreed to let someone sell you the stock at $15. (We'll just use the $15 strike price for the balance of this example.)

If the stock stays below $15, you will get it put to you. But think: your cost basis is $11.50 because you received $3.50 from the put premium. You bought the stock wholesale.

If the stock goes above $15 (remember this is what you thought would happen), the put option becomes increasingly worthless–you get to keep the premium and you don't have to buy the stock. Why would they sell it to you for $15 if it can be sold on the open market for $16 or more?

OR BUY A CALL?

If you think the stock is going up, why not buy a call option? My standard answer is, "You can do that too." Think about it. You've bought a call and sold a put on the same stock. Why both, or why sell the put? Simply because selling generates income. Buying costs money. It's a way of getting more cash into your account quickly.

The only hang-up is this: many beginners reading this chapter will not be allowed to sell naked puts (a covered put would be a situation where you're in a short position on the underlying stock) until you have more experience and/or more cash in your account. You see, you have the obligation to perform if the stock is put to you so your broker will require you to keep that amount of money (or 10 to 20% plus if you are on margin) on hold until the expiration date.

Selling puts generates income and lets you buy the stock wholesale.

If you are just getting started, you may want to stick to call options. I did and it worked for me quite nicely. But once you get familiar with rolls, peaks and valleys, and predictable stock movements, the put option tool gives you a way to truly enhance your income stream. Indeed, you can make twice as much as you catch the stock coming and going.

8

HOW TO GET A FREE RIDE...SORT OF

How would you like to get your stock investments for nothing? I'm not saying nothing down, but nothing, as in zero, zilch, nada. If you had no money tied up in an option purchase and you made $8,000, what would your rate of return be? For the answer to this question, figure out the answer to this division problem: $8,000 divided by 0 = ?. You say, "You can't divide by zero." Exactamundo. If you understand this, your work in real life will take on new meaning. The stars will shine brighter, your marriage will be happier, your kids will mind you, and you'll golf a 68.

SOMETHING FOR NOTHING

Something for nothing? Sounds impossible. Well, there are many wild and crazy impossibilities coming down everyday. This chapter is full of possibilities—infinite possibilities. As a matter of fact, the rate of return above is infinite because you can't divide anything into nothing. It is physically impossible to divide nothing into something. Go ahead— try!

Let's talk money. You calculate a rate of return based on dividing the profits (gain) by your cash in or cash on hold. A $1,200 profit on a $10,000 investment is 12%. That's simple. Now let's take on a hard one. A $1,200 profit on a zero dollar investment produces an infinite rate of return. The trick, my dear Sherlock, is getting $1,200 out of nothing.

Would you like to know that it's just not that tough? We're not going to defy gravity or any other law of nature. We'll just defy the laws of stodgy-thinking, Wall Street insiders who are helplessly locked into boring investment strategies. We are going to take all or some of our profits and buy or continue to own some of the stock. It's that simple, and while not exactly free, it has that semblance.

MULTIPLE OPPORTUNITIES

There are many opportunities in stock and option investing to get a free ride–ownership of an investment that cost nothing. It may have taken a shrewd play to make the profits needed to now have ownership in an option or stock with no outlay–or, at least having all your initial investment returned and ready to go to work again. The process of making back your initial outlay and then using profits to stay in the game is "Infinity Investing." Remember, you cannot divide by zero. It is physically impossible. If you have no cash tied up, you can't lose–except to the extent that you have an opportunity lost, in that your money might have done better elsewhere. Obviously, there is a cost because you could have moved the money elsewhere. Your cost is "what else could you have done?"

For the strategies in this chapter, we begin with the assumption that your trades in stocks or in options (whether calls or puts) have grown in value, at least enough of an increase to cover the spread between bid and ask–in short, to be profitable. Now, we are going to sell all or part of the investment. What we do with this profit and the calculated returns is our topic. Let's start with stocks.

WHY DID YOU BUY?

For this next section to make sense you need to know why you bought the stock.

Was it…

1. A new start-up and/or a new IPO?

2. A bottom fishing stock, i.e. one having a serious dip in price?

3. A rolling stock and you know the roll range (the channel between support and resistance)?

4. Purchased for a covered call strategy?

5. A high-quality stock added to your portfolio for strength?

If you don't know why you got involved, it will be difficult to ascertain the best time to sell. Indeed, except for the last point above, in all the other strategies the "exit" is more important than the "entrance." Remember, my rock-bottom trading strategy is to build up your cash flow.

This last statement has gotten me into hot water with a lot of traditionalists around the country. There are the investment clubs, the old-time brokerages, and even journalists who can't bring themselves to try anything new. The Warren Buffett philosophy is rampant. Don't get me wrong, I love his strategy. After you have mastered your own cash flow strategies and have built up your income, start concentrating on building a solid portfolio of "keepers."

Two points:

1. If you have a substantial portfolio and seriously want more income, then take a few thousand dollars and try more aggressive strategies. Call it play money. Note: Most of our Wall Street Workshop™ attendees with substantial assets make more profits by taking $5,000 of their $100,000 and investing it in rolling stocks, rolling options, option plays on stock splits, slams, peaks, et cetera, than they make on the other $95,000. Sure their $95,000 is safe and growing nicely. Just think, $95,000 at 10% will produce just under $10,000. But, I've seen a lot of people (too many to count) take $5,000 and make over $250,000 a year. And not quite so obvious, this is actual cash flow, not just an increase in value. It' time to head for the Bahamas.

Dear Mr. Cook:

Approximately fifteen to twenty years ago I attended your "Real Estate Money Machine" seminar where I learned your principles of buying real estate, fixing it up and selling it for a nice profit. To date, I am still using these principles and am experiencing wonderful results.

Five years ago I heard you on our local Christian radio station. You caught my attention when you said you were now making more money in the stock market than you did in real estate. At this point I decided to try your newest program.

I wasn't able to attend the Wall Street Workshop™ because of my Father's poor health, but I purchased the videotapes of the seminars. They were excellent. My first month I started with $2,900 and made $3,357 which was a 116% profit. I've been learning and trading ever since.

Recently, I've been following a stock, IDC (Inter Digital Communication) you've traded on W.I.N.™ I started buying options this fall when the stock was about $6 a share and by December 31st it closed at 74⁵/₈. This move made the options explode! My investment in November 99 of $30,000 in various IDC options grew to $2,421,000. I also traded a second account that went from $18,489 on December 15th to $385,363 by December 31st. This was only a two-week time frame. On my single best day the account values went from $1,028,000 on December 29th to $2,323,969 on December 30th. This was an increase of $1,295,969 in one day. On December 28th and 29th, I purchased 173 Jan 25 calls at an average price of 3¹/₂ ($60,454) and sold them on December 30th (two days later) at an average price at 33³/₈ (after commissions-$637,400) for a net profit of $576,945. This was a return of 954% in two days. I was ecstatic with these results. I want to thank you for your techniques, which gave me the knowledge and confidence to use your strategies. Without your videotapes I would not have these outstanding profits. Thank you.

—GLENN M., IL

2. If you only have a few thousand to invest, then you may want to throw caution to the wind and go for the gusto. If that's

where you are in your life and you want to generate income quickly, most mutual funds, stocks, and bonds will not respond fast enough. It's time to put a formula (system, recipe) to work and quickly "get in and get out." It's the *formula* that works, not a particular stock.

Your Vantage Point

This concept will not become real to you without the following two aspects.

1. You know going into an investment exactly what you want out of it.

2. You have purchased your investment wholesale—on a serious low in the stock (and, hence, the option).

Let's get on to a real life example. When you get to the option section, coming up in a few pages, this will get even more exciting.

You buy a stock for $8. It has been as high as $20. It's been down to $6. Lately it's been trading between $7 and $11. You buy 1,000 shares for $8,000. It takes three months, but the stock goes to $12. You value is $12,000.

Now, should you...

1. Sell it all and then hope it goes back down, and then buy in again?

A little voice speaks up: "But what if it goes to $30? After all, that's what the analysts say."

or

2. Hold on?

Another little voice speaks up, "But what if it goes back to $7?"

or

3. Sell part of it—in fact recapturing all your investment, then ride the remainder to greater returns?

Fireworks, orchestra, fanfare–bingo!– You've Got It!

Sell 700 shares at $12. That generates $8,400. After taking out commissions for both trades, you should have your $8,000 back, and look what you've done–the impossible. You own 300 shares of a $12 stock for zippo. Hopefully, this stock is in a great company. You have your cash back and 300 shares with no cash tied up.

I told you it wasn't that complicated or difficult. And there are still even greater things to think about. Before I delve into these, I'd like to discuss a point. Many people, I'm sure, have thought of this, or at least, have done it intuitively. Most powerful ideas are really quite simple.

I'm reminded of the story of the teacher who told all her first grade students that their drawing assignment that day was whatever they wanted to draw. As she was walking around the room checking on their progress, she saw one girl drawing intently. She asked what she was drawing. The youngster replied, "I'm drawing a picture of God."

"But no one knows what God looks like," the teacher said.

"They will when I get done," the girl said.

When you have profits now paying for your investment, and all your cash is out, then several things need to be discussed.

1. You can take your cash and wait, and buy this same stock on a dip. Maybe next time, you'll get 1,000 more shares at $7.

2. You can take your cash and buy a different, more promising opportunity.

3. The stock you still own (300 shares) is available for:

    a. Selling at a higher price.

    b. Writing a covered call–generating more income.

    c. Holding a good stock, thereby increasing your margin account. 300 shares at $12 is $3,600. This could turn into $7,200 (on margin)–or another $3,600 in buying power.

4. If the stock goes down, it is not fun, but it didn't cost you anything.

5. If it goes up to the $20 range you could sell all of it, or part of it. Selling all would generate another $6,000.

No one knows what the picture will look like. You can draw it yourself, but you should also know what you want it to look like before you start drawing. Stay a step ahead by knowing what your investments will do for you.

What if you ignore this last piece of advice? What if you don't know why you purchased the stock? What if you purchased it just because your stockbroker told you to? What if you didn't check the charts to see the highs and lows, the incline or decline, the range and time it takes to move from support to resistance? What if you haven't the foggiest idea of why you're in this stock?

Then how do you know when to get out, or buy more, or sell off part? You've got to know your exit before you go in the entrance!

One more point. If you know about this particular company, you've tracked its earnings, growth, et cetera and you still like it—you still think it has potential, then:

1. The 300 shares you own may prove profitable.

2. You could buy call options at $10, $12.50 or $15. Again, use some profit (maybe sell 50 or 100 more shares) to buy these options.

3. If you wait for another dip, your chance of increasing your next returns will be quicker.

4. You could sell puts (see the chapter on selling puts) for more cash flow.

5. If you think the $12 is a high and it's going to go down, you could buy puts and sell them as they get profitable.

But what if the story (where you think the stock is heading) isn't very good? Yes, there's a chance it might go up and your 300 shares may be more valuable, but if the story line has lost its momentum, then looking for similar opportunities elsewhere may be more profitable.

By the way, a lot of people find my tapes and seminars very helpful when beginning to trade, or when learning to trade options. If you feel like you'd like some more information on the topics covered in this chapter, or in any of the other chapters in this book, please call the 1-800 number on the back of the book. We've put together some helpful free audio cassettes (or CDs) about these same stock market investment and asset protection strategies that I think are really great.

A lot of people tell me I'm crazy giving this kind of information away for free instead of writing another book and making people buy it. But I don't write books to make most of my money. I make most of my money from trading and doing business. I write books and give seminars because I truly believe that this is the kind of trading information everyone should be getting already from their stockbrokers or other financial advisors.

Anyway, look at the three graphs and explanations on the following page. They are staggered to prove a point. As the door closes on one opportunity it opens on another.

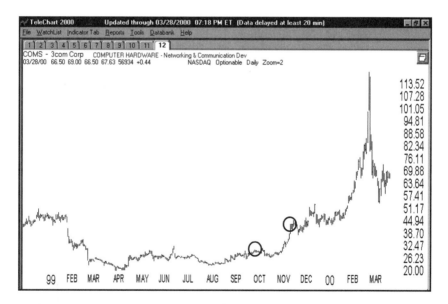

First we bought calls on 3Com (COMS) when the stock was at $28 (9/30/99). We sold when the stock hit $40 (11/22/99).

Then we bought options on Harmonics (HLIT) when the stock was at $70 (11/22/99). When HLIT moved up to $90 (12/22/99), we moved into Texas Instruments (TXN) at $106 (12/30/99) and got out at $130 (2/7/00).

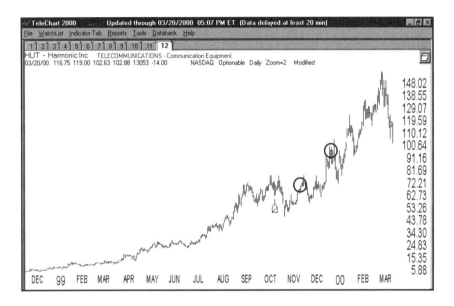

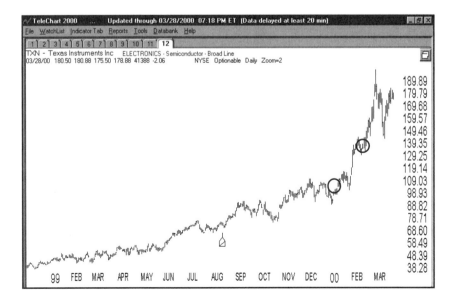

Each time profits are created it gives you an opportunity for another free ride.

OPTIONS: PROXY INVESTING

Options (calls and puts) on stocks open up all kinds of infinity-type returns and many ways to earn a free ride.

This is not the place to discuss all the aspects of options, but a few things are important to this discussion. Options allow you to control a large amount of stock with relatively small amounts of money. Also, small movements in the stock usually produce magnified movements in the option. Simply put, you can double, even triple your money, a lot faster. With these profits, a whole plethora of opportunities open up.

Remember though, we purchased the option for a specific purpose and at/for a specific time.

1. *Call Options* (We think the stock will rise).

   The stock is...

   a. rolling

   b. on a dip (slam, bottom fishing)

   c. doing a split

   d. coming out with news

2. *Put Options* (We think the stock will go down).

   The stock has...

   a. bad news

   b. a reverse split

   c. peaked out–run up on good news, unsustainable

   d. come within a few days of the split date (give or take two to eight days)

Let's stick with call options for this example. Put options are the same, but in reverse. The above is for *purchasing* calls and puts. Selling them is a whole different story.

The stock is at $40. It has traded as high as $50 and has been down to $38. You think it has potential. It seems to have bottomed out in the high $30 to low $40 range. It's August. You purchase 10 contracts of the October $40 calls for $3.75; your cost is $3,750. You also purchase 10 contracts of the January $45 calls for $5.25. Total outlay is $5,250. By September 8 the stock is at $44. Your October $40 calls are $6.25, or $6,250. The January options are up also, but because they're further out they haven't moved as much. They are $6–still a $1,750 profit.

Now what do you do? Check again why you bought the options. If you're following the Wade Cook method, it was not to purchase 2,000 shares of this stock. But wait. What do I see? A nice quick profit–extra cash generated in hours or days.

Look what you can do with these profits. Let's just deal with the October calls.

1. Continue to hold for greater profits.

2. Sell some–say eight contracts for $6.25. That's about $5,000. We have all our cash back and we can even take some profits and buy more options on this stock or other stocks. In this case we would only have to sell seven to recover our investment and get a *free ride* on the other three.

Note: If this run-up of $4 (10% of the stock price) had occurred in a one or two-day period, I'd probably sell all of the options. Barring additional news, most of these quick spurts are not sustainable. Sell, and then buy back in on a dip at an expiration date a little further out. The October options were purchased in August. If it's now mid-September we should probably look at the November or December options.

3. Sell all or part of the options and buy some of this stock.

This point is very important to me. I've written on it elsewhere but it is also appropriate here. I am big into building a solid portfolio of well-run companies with good earnings and hopefully increasing earnings. I like companies with expansion dynamics at work. Most people who read my books and come to my seminars need more cash flow. They, like me in the beginning, need a more aggressive approach with a small amount of money. They need to develop their own money machine.

Then they should diversify into real estate, gold, or other investments like small businesses, energy resources, et cetera. The stock market is too risky for all your money to be in one basket. Some of this diversification could be into stocks in great companies–even recession-proof companies. Get back to fundamentals and doing your homework.

Speaking of homework, part of the homework you did to decide if you wanted this option in the first place–and which option (strike price, expiration date), will now help you decide if you should buy or sell this stock, or hold on to it.

Remember, if we've sold 10 October contracts for $6.25, that's $6,250, of which $2,500 is profit. Yes, we could take all of this money ($6,250) and buy more options, but if you follow this thought, your portfolio will be full of risk. Options expire. Be careful. A downturn in the market could wipe out a substantial part of your assets.

Let's use all of the $2,500, or even half of it, and buy some stock. If you like the $44 stock, buy 10 shares, or 50, or even 100. One hundred shares would cost $4,400, but only $2,200 on margin.

You're free riding again. Your $2,500 is put to a good, yes boring, but still a good use. Use your $3,750 (your option/profit seed money) for your next quick play.

There is an advantage to owning stock in a lot of companies. One is that shareholders receive news from the companies: updates, reports, and shareholder voter information. Get them and read them. You're learning about earnings, expansion plans, stock splits, changes in management, et cetera. Part of good investment habits is to get, and act upon, good and timely information. Shareholders get this all the time.

MORE OPTIONS

If you want to play more options on this same company, consider the following:

Wait for dips–be patient. Study the charts and pick the most opportune strike price and expiration date.

Sell out, take your profits, and buy back in at a higher strike price. Once again, the assumption has to be that the stock will increase.

Opportunities keep knocking when you have no cash tied up and have purchased an investment at bargain prices.

Selling the option when it is profitable opens up another possibility. If you sell part of your position, and if you think the stock has peaked (you still own a few call options) then buy a put with the profit. You now have created a straddle for *free*.

A pure straddle is one where you own calls and puts on the same stock, at the same strike price, and for the same month. Your straddle does not have to be pure. You can buy a call at one strike price, and buy a put at another strike price.

Either way, as the stock moves up you sell the call, as the stock moves down you sell the put. You get something for nothing. I can't add more. It's a great way to enhance your cash flow and/or add to your portfolio.

9

KNOWING WHEN TO SELL

Never before has it taken so long for me to write a chapter. I've had my notes ready, with few additions, for months. Why? Because this information is so vital, so pertinent, that I wanted plenty of time to think and formulate answers to all the questions I get about the timing of sell points.

HOW TO KNOW WHEN TO SELL

I have given a lot of this information elsewhere–bits and pieces here, brief explanations there. It is probably the most visited area of all my seminars and personal meetings: "When do I get out (sell)?" I think people ask me this because from my real estate days on I've advocated several generalized exit strategies, including:

1. Know your exit before you go in the entrance.

2. You capitalize your profits when you sell.

I've also made remarks like the following: "It's easy to get into business; it's hard to get out. It's easy to buy real estate; it's hard to sell. It's easy to get into personal relationships with people; it's hard to get out. It's always easier to get in than to get out, but you make your money when you get out. Sure, you have to buy right going in (and if you do you'll make a profit), but again, you get the cash (or cash flow) when you sell."

Also, I mentioned to people at my real estate seminars that I felt sorry for them if they asked me a question about a problem they were having with their properties because I only had one answer: sell.

The reader must also understand my "cab driver" mentality background.

1. The money is made in the meter drop™. You make more by ending one run quickly and getting on to the next. I know this is contrary to all the current advice. I, too, buy and hold some stocks and options (LEAPS®). But the cash flow comes from buying and selling–trading, and getting on to the next deal.

2. There's always another cab (or bus or train). I once read an old Irish proverb that makes sense here: "the biggest fish you'll ever catch is still swimming in the ocean." I'll add, "you've got to be out fishing to catch it."

Remember, my style is to turn the stock market into a business. No business buys inventory to keep. The profits are in the selling process.

With all of this in mind, let me move on to the strategies that have helped me. Remember, I use various formulas and processes, rules, if you will, to get me in and out. Each has a distinctive nature, and the rules are only occasionally the same. For example, selling a call on a covered call play is totally different than selling stock on a rolling stock play.

This chapter is about exiting. Obviously there will be more on getting into the stocks in the various other chapters on these formulas.

Let's start with my old favorite, rolling stock.

ROLLING STOCK

This one is easy because you can run a chart (go back six months, a year, or even five years) and see the peaks and valleys. You look at the high point (it's formally called "resistance") and put your order in to sell at that point or just below that point. Remember: don't get greedy.

A stock may roll between $3 and $4.50, but it only hits $4.50 once in a while. Put your order in to sell at $4.25. You'll probably want to put in a "Good Till Canceled" (GTC) order (and renew it if the sixty-day limit expires). Look at the following charts:

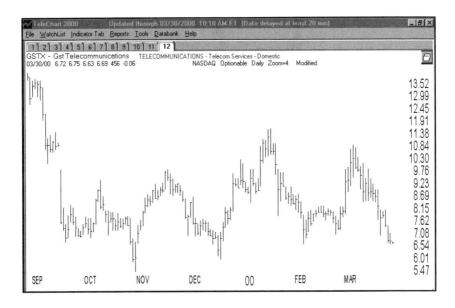

You can see in GST Telecommunications (GSTX) that the roll range changes. Most people freak out if the stock goes down—especially after they just bought it. Only once in a while have I been burned by this. You see, you have two choices. Look at a changing roll pattern with Cineplex Odeon (CPX).

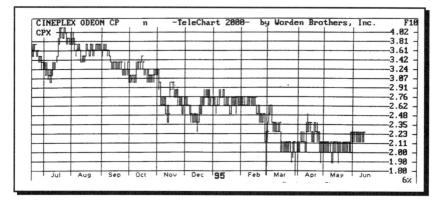

For years (this is a one year chart) it has gone between $2.50 and $3.50. Then it dropped to $1.50. I had just purchased 2,000 shares at $2.50 and then another 2,000 at $2 when it dropped to the $1.50 range. It even hit $1.25 once or twice. Now the two choices:

1. Just wait it out. It may take several months for it to get back up to $3 or $3.50. But at least you won't lose.

2. Hang on to what you have and wait to see if it establishes a new roll range. A variation of this is to look for a significant bottom, a real support, and a genuine move back up in the stock. That's what I did. I bought some at $1^3/8$ and $1^1/2$ and sold most at $1^7/8$ and a little at $2. It went back to $1^1/2$ or so, and I bought back in.

As we were going to press with this chapter it looked like Cineplex Odeon (CPX) was establishing a new roll range. I'll make more cash flow on quick rolls than anything I'd lose on the dip in value of the 4,000 shares. Plus, I still have the 4,000 shares with two more choices:

1. Continue to hang on.

2. Sell, take the loss, and get the cash moving on this lower roll range, or invest elsewhere.

YOUR ORDER TO SELL

You can either place a GTC order and forget about it, or you can watch it closely and sell at an optimum time. Which method you use depends upon you; more specifically, on how busy you are. If you're really busy, just place the GTC order and get on with your other business. If you have ample time, you'll probably make more by watching the stock and figuring out the best time to sell.

Also note, on any given day the stock could move in tandem with the whole stock market. At least it could give it an extra 25¢ to 50¢ of profitability. For example: Let's say a stock is rolling between $3 and $4. It hits $4.50 once in a while. You have a GTC order to sell at $4. The past few days it has run up quickly to $3.75 and the market is strong. Consider canceling your GTC order and watch it, or change it to $4.25 or $4.50. No, it's not getting greedy, it's just smart. The economy, or good news, or an up move in the Dow could drive it up to its high or even beyond.

Conversely, a down market may drive the price to $2.50 or $2.75. If you buy now, you pick up an extra 25¢ to 50¢ when you sell at $4. It's not only a bargain, but a super bargain.

In December of 1995, I had been intrigued by the reported returns in the mailers from [Stock Market Institute of Learning]. I had not made a commitment to attend the Wall Street Workshop™ but decided to "just try" a rolling stock strategy to see if it really worked. Wade had touted Cineplex Odeon (CPX) as a rolling stock. January 4th 1996, I bought (on margin) 2,000 shares of CPX at $1¹/₂ and placed an order to sell at $2¹/₂.

A month later, I was less excited when they hadn't reached $2¹/₂ and I adjusted my sell per share to $2. I decided to attend the Chicago Wall Street Workshop™ in June. While I was there, CPX increased to $2 and my sell order was executed. The results were great.

—STEVEN M.

Note: Cineplex Odeon was taken over and is now called Loews Cineplex. I'll put the new chart of Loews (LCP) here. Compare the difference with the old Cineplex Odeon (CPX) chart on the previous page. This chart represents a reverse range rider pattern.

ALL OR PART

You can also sell part of your position at one price and part at another. If you bought 1,000 shares at $3, you could place your GTC order on 500 shares at $4 and 500 shares at $4.25.

This is obviously personal to you. I can't begin to tell you what to do, just as I can't tell you all the ramifications of what you can do.

ROLLING OPTIONS

Exiting a position on rolling options is quite similar to a plain rolling stock play. If you find a stock that rolls (channels) within a certain range, and if the stock is optionable, then as it hits its low point you purchase a call option at the next higher strike price. If it's a stock under $25, you may want to purchase it two strike prices higher.

EXAMPLE

A stock rolls between $18 and $22. When it gets to $18 and bottoms out, purchase the $20 call. Its price is 62.5¢. Ten contracts would cost $625. Now wait or put in your GTC order to sell. Try to guess when to get out. After you've done it several times you'll just know a good exit point. If the stock hits $21 (remember don't get greedy) and the option then goes for $1.50, you could sell for $1,500 and have a cool $875 profit. Nice and predictable.

If the stock has frequently bumped against, and even gone over $22.50 (the next higher strike price), you may want to purchase the option at that strike price. It would be really cheap if the stock were $18. How does 12.5¢ ($^1/_8$) sound? If you go to the next higher strike price, you should probably consider going out one or two additional months. Instead of 12.5¢ the option may be 37.5¢, but that additional quarter may well be worth it. And frankly, the stock may need more time to get close to, or over, the $22.50 strike price.

Realize also, you're not doing this to buy the stock. You're doing this play to wait for an increase in the value of your option so you can sell at a profit. Now where do you sell? Probably the same place as before—in the $21 plus range. It won't take too much of a move for you to double or even triple your money. And again you could have a GTC order in place or watch and wait and sell at an optimum time.

THE WAY DOWN

If you choose to purchase puts on the way down, do everything in reverse. Wait for the stock to peak out, check for other news, including where the market in general is heading (don't fight trends), and buy a put. Sell it as the stock decreases in value. On a $25 stock, purchase the $22.50 put or even consider the $25 or $20. The $25 put will cost more because it's in the money, but you have some insurance. The $20 (or lower) strike price will cost less because it's way out of the money. Pick an exit point that you're comfortable with and upon selling the put, watch for the true bottom (or support level) to sell the put, then jump back in with a call option and ride it back up. Keep the cycle going.

DATE (EXPIRATION FRIDAY, NOV. 19)	STOCK PRICE	OPTION PRICE ON $25 CALL
Oct. 20	26.00	1.75
Oct. 25	27.00	3.00
Oct. 30	28.00	4.25
Nov. 5	29.00	5.50
Nov. 10	31.00	6.75
Nov. 15	32.00	7.625
Nov. 17	33.00	8.25
Nov. 19	34.00	9.125

I took the Wall Street Workshop™ in October of 1995. I bought options in a few companies and was ahead at the end of the year by a little over $9,000. You know, this year has been thrilling. My gains thus far in 1996 exceed $86,000! All of your courses have been wonderful, but your Wall Street Workshop™ has been the most rewarding financially. Thank you.

—SANDI, WA

OPTIONS: THREE GENERAL SELL POINTS

A quick explanation would be in order. A stock option gives you a chance to purchase or sell an underlying stock. It's not a pure gamble in that you can actually act on the underlying security. Small movements in the underlying stock can produce, on a percentage basis, drastic moves in the option. I've seen a stock move up $3 and an option on that stock move up $2.50. You ask, so what? Well the stock went from $74 to $77. The $70 call option went from $5.25 to $7.75. Talk about a great proxy investment. The same can happen with puts.

Investors buy options for:

1. Maximum bang for your buck—the expiration month and various strike prices should be analyzed.

2. Quick return on your money.

Again, we're not here to discuss entrance strategies. You can read about those elsewhere. I only bring this up as a lead in to the next point. Is time a friend or foe? If we want to get out at not just a nice profit but at the best possible profit, we need to explore this question.

An option may be comprised of two parts: intrinsic value and time value. Intrinsic value is that portion of the option that is in the money. Time value is that portion of the option that is out of the money. For example, if the stock is $26 and the $25 call options are going for $1.75, $1 of the $1.75 is intrinsic value and the 75¢ of the $1.75 purchase price is time value. The 75¢ pays for one week, or two months, or whatever time is left before the expiration date.

The reason I said "may" at the beginning of the last paragraph is that the option may be all time value. If you're after the $30 strike price, the stock is at $26, and the option is 50¢, the whole 50¢ is time value. Time value could be called extrinsic value, as it is extrinsic to the value of the stock.

At first, time is a friend. Your 75¢ has purchased you a month and a half–six weeks. If the stock rises, the option value increases. You could sell at anytime. If you had purchased a call option with a $30 strike

STOCK PRICE	DATE (EXPIRATION DATE FRI, NOV 19)	OPTION PRICE ($30 CALL)
26.00	Oct. 20	0.50
27.00	Oct. 25	0.75
27.50	Oct. 30	1.00
28.00	Nov. 5	1.25
28.00	Nov. 10	1.25
28.25	Nov. 12	1.375
28.50	Nov. 14	1.50
28.75	Nov. 15	1.50
29.00	Nov. 16	1.75
29.25	Nov. 17	1.75
29.375	Nov. 18 Thurs.	1.50
25.43	Nov. 18 noon Thurs.	1.37
29.50	Nov. 19 Fri.	0.75
29.50	Nov. 19 noon Fri.	0.25
29.50	Expiration	worthless

price, the option value increases up to a point. If the stock goes above $30, you've made a nice play and you can get out at a nice profit.

If, however, the stock moves toward $30 and you've seen a nice run up in your option, but then the stock stalls, you may want to be careful. Time becomes the enemy. The option (stock) needs time to move up, and more specifically, move to the strike price, or it may become worthless.

Look at the previous diagram. Note the dates. Notice how in the last few days before the expiration date the stock is still going up a little but the option goes nowhere and then down. Time runs out. We're purchasing the November $30 call options for 50¢.

Do you see how fast the time value deteriorates when there is no time left? As you look at this diagram you can obviously see several exit points where you could have made a nice profit. Also note that the time value of in-the-money calls evaporates as you get near the expiration date. Look at the next diagram. This is the $35 call option. The stock starts at $26.

Sometimes we, "tongue in cheek," refer to time value as fluff. When there is ample time before the expiration date, the time value portion of the option premium is large. In the above example it was 75¢ back on October 20, but only 25¢ two days before the November 19 expiration date.

STOCK PRICE	DATE (EXPIRATION FRI., NOV. 19TH)	OPTION PRICE
$26	Oct. 20	$0.75
27	Oct. 25	1.00
28	Oct. 30	0.75
29	Nov. 5	0.75
31	Nov. 10	0.50
32	Nov. 15	0.25
33	Nov. 17	0.25
34	Nov. 18	0.125

There comes a time when you get less bang for your buck. I would have sold this option at a double or triple. Be careful. If it gets to be November 10 and the stock takes a two-dollar dip, the value can erode very quickly.

When the stock has less time to recover it may not regain its previous value. A lot of money can be made in the expiration week but only for someone with a stout heart. I hope you see how easily the "friend" can quickly turn to "foe."

OUT OF YOUR OPTIONS

There are four major strategies for determining when to get out of options. I'll cover these as I blend in specific formulas on option plays. We'll look at:

1. Peaks

2. Slams ("Dead Cat Bounce")

3. Ninety-degree angles

4. Covered Calls

5. Selling Calls

6. Selling Puts

7. Stock Splits

GET OUT WHEN YOU WOULDN'T GET IN

A lot of your investing will come down to how you feel. Your fears may keep you out of trouble. Your desire to get in when you hear great news will usually help you get great results. For example, all your research says a stock could hit $30 in a short time. It's currently $20. If it gets close to $28 you may want to sell. If you had purchased the $25 call option (or even the $30 option) and it's had a nice run, check the news, see if there's more potential upside, and consider selling. If the stock is at $30 and no new news has come out, definitely sell.

Remember options have a short life. If you own the stock you could hang on and wait for the next earnings report or whatever. You don't want the option to expire. Sell it and then buy back in at a higher strike price; or wait for weakness and buy back in at the same strike price—just out another month or two; or take your money elsewhere.

The point is this: if you wouldn't buy the stock or option at a certain price, and you do in fact own it, then sell it at that point where you wouldn't buy it. That sell point is your best-guess summation.

A variation of this point is using the "percent to double," or points to double rule, which I've written about in the *Wall Street Money Machine, Volume 1*. We use the "%Dbl" to determine if buying an option is a good deal. Many brokers can get access to the on-line computer services that have this program. It's a computer model whose "bottom line" tells us how much a stock would have to move for us to double our money on a particular option. I like low percentage movements (under 10%)—take a quick profit and get out.

Let's say a stock is $82. The $90 strike price on the call option is $2.50 and the percent to double is 6%. The stock (at this particular point in time) would have to go up almost $5 for our $2.50 to double to $5 (6% of $82 = about $5). If the stock has an upward trend or good news, et cetera, then this could be a great play. Remember, your $2.50 option doesn't have to go up double for you to make a nice profit. A 50¢ move would be nice, especially if it's in a few days.

The point though, in this chapter is not to determine when to get in, but when to get out. If the stock and option have an upward move, check the %Dbl. If it's high, say 13%, then you should sell. Think of it: you probably wouldn't buy an option with a 13% to double. Back to our example, if the stock has moved to $88 and our $2.50 option is $4, and at this point (time remaining and other factors involved) it would require a $10 move to take the $4.50 to $9, then you may want to sell for the $4.50.

You'll probably get your biggest profits shortly after you've bought in at a really low price, then get out on a quick up-tick in the stock.

KNOW YOUR EXIT BEFORE ENTERING

I don't want to wear out this concept, but for many plays it's very important. Here we'll deal with a few option plays. We've already covered rolling options. Let's now cover a peak or a slam.

PEAKS

When a stock has a tremendous run up, say in one day it goes from $52 to $63, because of good news, unless there's more good news coming out, it will probably back off. If you own the call options, get out. If you want to get in and play the downturn, buy puts on the stock and ride it back down. If the increase stalls, or even comes down a little, you could sell the options and buy back in on the dip.

If you own the stock you could also write a covered call, and again, ride it back down. You collect the premium and you also keep the stock.

SLAMS

When a stock takes a hit, you could buy a call and get out with a profit in hours. Here's how it works. The company comes out with lower than expected earnings (it's still highly profitable, but not up to what analysts expected). The stock falls from $62 to $54. The next day it finds support and even goes back up to $55. Consider buying the short-term option and purchasing the $55 call. It needs to be close. It's going for $2. (*Note:* The $50 call is $6: $5 in the money and $1 time value. This costs more but may be a better play. Think it through.) A move to $56 or $57 could easily drive your $2 option to $3. Then get out.

You could have gone further out (two to four months) on the $55 call or the $60 call, but that was not this play. This is short term. You should have placed the order to sell at $3 (especially if you can't sit and watch it) right after you purchased it for $2. You know your exit before buying.

I have covered exit strategies on covered and uncovered calls and on selling puts elsewhere. I'll only add this here: they are options. They have a fixed life. If you've sold a call or put and generated cash, you have two choices.

1. Let the option expire and keep the cash.

2. If the option shrinks significantly and you think the stock might bounce, then you could buy back the option and sell it again as it gets more profitable.

The best "out" enhancement strategy is to have gotten in at a bargain in the first place.

GET OUT WHEN YOU'RE HAPPY

I know this sounds ambiguous but it's important to realize that there is not just one time to get out. If you have invested $2,000 in ten contracts of a $2 option and one hour later it shoots up to $3 or $3,000, you have an hour profit of $1,000. If *you're happy*, then get out. Take your profits and go to a movie.

Of course you shouldn't get out if there's more potential, but if this was initiated as a quick play, then take your profits and look for another deal–dips, new stock splits, et cetera. So what if it goes to $4. The next day it could be at 50¢.

Stocks and options are like ocean waves. They ebb in, they flow out. Nothing stays the same.

> *This is to let you know that during the five business days following the Wade Cook Wall Street Workshop™, I averaged approximately $250 a day using only the covered calls technique I learned during the workshop. In addition, by working with a full-service broker, I was able to obtain a very good position in an IPO with excellent potential for a 100% gain on my money. Additionally, using the margin concept, I was able to obtain 500 shares of a strong "takeover" stock for a possible 30–40% profit.*
>
> *All things considered, I am confident I have started on a realistic course to financial independence. Thanks to all in [Seattle] for their time and expertise. Wade was correct when he said the workshop is worth more than ten times the tuition amount.*
>
> —RICHARD S., WA

WATCH AND GET OUT

Most of my stockbrokers are so busy they won't do this strategy, however, the ones who really watch out for my best interests, will.

Let's say a stock is having a nice run up. You are quite profitable on your option, but want to get out at maximum profit. Ask your stockbroker to keep an eye on it. If it peaks and you can catch it at or near the peak, then you can get out with an even greater return.

An example: the stock was at $80 after a slam, or other bad news, or even after good news. It goes to $81. You call your stockbroker and buy the $80 calls for $3 and the $85 calls for $1.25. The stock goes to $83, then $84, and one hour before the market closes it's at $85—almost $86. The stock hangs around $86, seems to have stalled, backs off to $85.50 with 10 minutes before the close—this is it—(yes, there is tomorrow, but this is today). Carpe diem. Seize the moment. Sell and take your profits. The $80 call is $6.25 and the $85 call is $3.75. That's a $3.25 profit on the $80's and a $2.50 profit on the $85's. It's been a nice day.

Yes, it may still go up tomorrow, but many times they fall back. This stock had a 3%, then 4%, then 5% run up in one day. Surely I can't tell you what to do, but I usually take my profits and wait for another dip.

Two more points:

1. The options market closes a few minutes after the stock market. If you are willing to buy at the ask and sell at the bid (buy or sell at the market), you can still trade options at 4:03 PM, 4:05 PM, sometimes even 4:06 PM (Eastern time). Why do I bring this point up here? Many times, stocks go up or down a few dollars right at the close. If the options have a corresponding move, you could get out at a higher price or get in at a lower price.

   However, unless there is really spectacular news (good or bad) which comes out overnight, the options are usually pretty much the same the next morning. Just once in a while, I do option trades after the stock market closes.

2. If you have a good profit you could sell part of your position and keep part active. You don't have to sell all of your contracts you've purchased. Sell part to capture some profits now and keep some to capture larger profits later.

You might even be profitable enough on the ones you've sold to regain all the money spent on all of your contracts–you now own the contracts you've kept, for free.

10

SELLING PUTS
(MY FAVORITE STRATEGY)

Some of you have heard me tell the story of a certain gentleman in one of my early seminars who was disagreeing with me and dominating the seminar for two full days. Finally, someone asked me, "Wade, what is the single best investment strategy you know of? Where can you generate the richest returns?"

I saw the chance to make a point, so I turned to my heckler and handed him the question. He said, "Easy. Sell puts."

And then I said, "I agree, but now aren't you people glad you paid me to teach you investment strategies instead of attending this man's seminar, because he would have spent two days teaching you to sell puts, and you would have gone home and discovered you couldn't do it. You can't sell puts until you have both a lot of experience and/or a substantial reserve of cash set aside in your account."

Well, people have always been grateful that we teach them 13 strategies at our seminars, which they can implement immediately to generate cash flow. Many of our students have done just that. In fact, they have gained so much experience and generated so much cash that they are ready now to sell puts! And so the time has come for this chapter.

THE BASICS OF SELLING PUTS

Selling puts is about cash flow and a rather unique way of getting it. Everyone has heard that you can make money in any market, but the people saying so fail to give details on how to do it. More specifically, "they" say you can make money whether a stock is going up or going down. I want to give some specifics on how to make money in options where the stock is increasing or decreasing in value. This is an option chapter. We will explore a cash flow generation strategy which will deal with stocks that you hope are going up–or will at least stay the same. Note: see the chapter "Tandem Plays" for doubling up these strategies.

Selling (naked) puts is a very unique and seldom-used strategy with a host of benefits. We will put some flesh on this skeleton, and some muscle, give it a brain, and put it to work for you.

Definitions are in order. Stock option investing gives an investor the right, but not the obligation to buy or sell a particular stock at a set price (strike price) on or before a certain date. Call options give the investor the right to buy a stock. These options can be bought or sold. Put options give the investor the right to sell a stock. These, too, can be bought or sold.

Strike prices for all options are the same. They start at $5, and go up by $2.50 increments to $25, in $5 increments to $200, and in $10 increments thereafter. Options are written in 100 share contracts. Hence, a 75¢ option will cost $75 for one contract. Options are derivatives. A derivative is a proxy investment based on an underlying security. Stock options are different than most derivatives in that the investor actually has the right to take control of (own by purchasing or selling) the underlying stock.

Options end–they expire. Because they are a fixed-time investment, investors should not only be wary and very cautious, but should invest in options by keeping an eye on the time clock. You may have the best horse on the track but if it falls behind or gets a bad start, the race may be over before it begins. The price of the option is broken into two parts. Part of the premium is actually purchasing the time until the option expires. This is called time value. If the stock price is above the strike price (call options) or below the strike price (put options), the option is said to be "in the money." The portion of the option that is in the money is called intrinsic value. I will use several examples and this definition will come to life. Understanding time value (extrinsic) and intrinsic value is not only important, but *sine qua non* to effectively making decisions on which option to purchase on a particular stock.

Put options, and a particular angle to using them, is the topic here. Let's keep exploring them. If you *purchase* a put option, you are thinking (hoping) that the stock will go down. What if, however, you don't think the stock is going down? In fact, you think the stock is a winner. Is buying the stock or buying a call option on the stock the only way to take advantage of an increasing stock value?

No, selling puts is another strategy that accomplishes two major objectives:

1. It generates new income.

2. If you have to buy the stock, it lets you buy wholesale.

There are other minor strategies that allow for even greater returns. We'll get to those later.

> *On Monday, July 8, I heard that Ascend Communications was going to announce their quarterly earnings this week. Well, I've been waiting for an opportunity to buy some shares. I have traded this stock many times and I know it is one of Wade's favorites. Lately the stock has broken its upward trend pattern and retreated from its high of $71.25 in late May. I felt this might be a good buy here in the $55 range, but still wanted to hedge a little. I would be delighted to buy the stock at around $50, so I decided to look at selling some $50 puts. The July $50 puts were around $1⅝, the September $50 puts were at $4½. The stock was now firming a little in anticipation of the earnings coming out. It looked like a very good play.*
>
> *I sold five contracts for the July $50 puts for $1⅝ and sold five (5) contracts of the September $50 puts for $4½. I was a little hesitant to go out to September, but I asked myself, what's*

*the worst that can happen? I would have to buy 500 shares of a
stock I want at cost basis of $45½ in September (before its next
earnings report). Sounds pretty good to me. (If this up trend continues as it has in the past, the stock could even split by then
anyway.)*

*So today, Wednesday, July 10, Ascend closed up $3¾. The
July $50 puts are now at $⅛ and the September $50 puts are
now at $3. I collected a premium of over $3,000 by selling these
puts, which is a lot cheaper than buying the stock outright and
trying to realize a $3,000 gain. There is really not much down-
side risk here.*

—T.E.

THE STRATEGY

Okay, here we go. A stock is at $13.50. You really like the com-
pany. You think this stock could easily go to $18 or $20. You think this
because:

1. The stock is rolling between $13 and $20, and has done so
   frequently. You know this from looking at its chart.

2. You have heard good news from the company–i.e., new products, expansion, great earnings, et cetera.

You could buy the stock or buy the $12.50, $15 or even $17.50 call
options. If the stock rises as expected, the value of your investments
increases. Both of these choices require an expenditure of money. If
you buy the stock on margin, you only have to put up a percentage of
the money (in most cases 50%). I bring this up here because margin
requirements will be necessary when selling puts–see the section on
"cash requirements."

Let's not buy the stock or call options. Let's sell a $15 put, or even
the $12.50 put, if you think the stock may go down further. What does
this mean? Let's use the $15 put example first. If you sell a $15 put, you
are literally committing yourself to buy the stock at $15. You no longer
have just the right (as in buying an option); you now have the obligation to perform if the stock gets "put to you." You can also end this

position by repurchasing the put at a profit or a loss–either way, you end the obligation to take the stock.

You see, by writing a put (selling), you have given someone the right to sell you the stock at $15. They don't know who you are–all they have done is purchase a put option–giving them the right, not the obligation, to sell the stock to someone at $15. When would they do this? When the stock is below $15. Now, if the stock is at $14.75 or $14.875 on the expiration date, it's iffy whether or not it will get put to you. (See "Selling Calls" in the *Wall Street Money Machine, Volume 1* for more information on the execution of these close orders.) However, if the stock is at $14 or $13 *it will get put to you* at $15.

What did you get for selling the put? When will you get the cash? The premium you receive is determined by how far the strike price is in the money or out of the money, and how long until it expires.

> *PC Docs Group International (DOCSG) closed at $16¹/4 today. This appears to be a stock that will return to its normal roll between $18 and $21 prior to August 12th. Moreover, the August $17¹/2 put price is quite favorable. Even if you were called to purchase the stock at $17¹/2 it would be a wholesale purchase which could be turned around at a profit in a relatively short time.*
>
> *I am an avid fan of W.I.N.™, and can't read Mr. Cook's book enough times.*
>
> —M.F., LA

As I was editing this book for reprint a great play developed. The stock was Terrim (TERN). It had risen from the $70 range last fall to $267. Rumors were out about the authorization of new shares–a sign of a potential stock split announcement. The $200 puts of March were going for $6. I sold ten contracts. It was February 25. The margin requirement would be 10%, or about $26,000. That is a $6,000 profit on a $26,000 margin hold, and all the stock has to do is stay above $200 for the next three weeks. Not a bad return. No spread was possible around these strike prices. I don't often do naked puts as many of my students can't do naked put sells, but this time I made an exception.

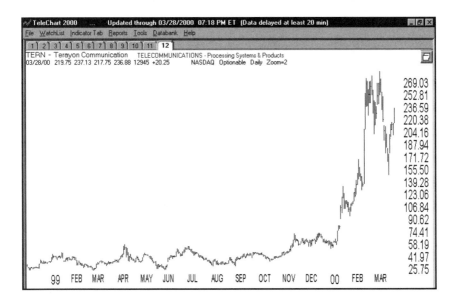

TeleChart 2000   ...   Updated through 03/28/2000 07:18 PM ET (Data delayed at least 20 min)

File WatchList Indicator Tab Reports Tools Databank Help

| 1 | 2 | 3 | 4 | 5 | 6 | 7 | 8 | 9 | 10 | 11 | 12 |

TERN - Terayon Communication   TELECOMMUNICATIONS - Processing Systems & Products
03/28/00 219.75 237.13 217.75 236.88 12945 +20.25   NASDAQ Optionable Daily Zoom=2

FIFTEEN DOLLAR PUT PLAY

If the stock is $13.50, you get at least $1.50 for the $15 put because that's how much the stock is in the money. Let's say you sell ten contracts. That will generate $1,500. However, that is all intrinsic value. Depending on the time to expiration, there will be added to this the time value, perhaps another 50¢. That's $2 or $2,000. The cash will be in your account the next trading day. You now are obligated to purchase 1,000 shares of this stock at $15. I'll discuss movement and what we have accomplished, but to do so we need to see the relationship between the stock and put option prices.

STOCK PRICE	STRIKE PRICE	OPTION PRICE
$12.50	$15.00	$3.50
13.00	15.00	2.75
13.50	15.00	2.00
14.00	15.00	1.25
15.00	15.00	0.75
15.50	15.00	0.25
16.00	15.00	0.125
17.00	15.00	No bid

Obviously, these prices are a snapshot in time. The option prices would be significantly higher if we went out several months, and significantly lower if the stock is not close to $15, or if it's just a few days until the expiration date.

Back to the strategy. Again, we have obligated ourselves to buy this stock at $15. We have made $2,000 cash and it is in our account. We now play the waiting game. The big question is this: Are we willing to buy the stock at $15, or do we want to buy the stock at all? If the answer is no, then you probably should not have sold the right to someone to sell it to you at $15. Simply put–you had better like this company, *and like it at that particular price*, or you should not have done this.

Okay, you have $2,000 cash in your account, now what do you want to happen? If you don't really want to buy the stock (which is my desire in about 99% of the cases where I've sold puts), but wouldn't mind, then you hope the stock goes up.

If the stock moves above $15, the stock won't get put to you and you get to keep the money ($2,000). Remember, that was a deciding factor–you thought this stock was going up.

If the stock doesn't perform this way, then you will now own the stock. It will be in your account, the Thursday after the third Friday of the expiration month. Before we explore briefly what you can do with the stock, let's look at what happened.

BUYING WHOLESALE

You just purchased this stock for $13. Your cost basis is adjusted by the premiums you've received from selling the put. If you've ever wanted to buy wholesale, you've done so. You've taken in $2 for selling the put. Your $15 purchase price is adjusted by this amount and you have a $13 cost basis. Just think, this stock could be selling at $14.50. You could take the stock and sell it immediately and have a $1,500 profit. You could also:

1. Hold onto the stock for awhile. Remember, you thought this stock was going up. Is the story line still true?

2. Sell a covered call on all or part of the stock. You could now sell a call option at a $12.50 or $15 strike price, or wait for the stock to strengthen and sell the $15 call option for more money (hoping to get called out or not), or even the $17.50 strike price if it moves up a lot.

3. Go short on the stock so you don't have to actually purchase it. I'll explain this later.

One thing I learned from my real estate days is that if you buy wholesale, all kinds of good choices present themselves. You can sell immediately and your payments are lower so you can rent at a profit, et cetera. The same is true with stocks. You have good choices if you buy wholesale.

OTHER BUY-BACK STRATEGIES

Long before we purchase the stock, and along the way as it is rising, there are still other things we can do to take advantage of the "magnified movement" in the option price. Review the previous diagram.

As the stock rises and gets close to the $15 strike price, the value of the put goes down. If it's awhile before the expiration date and the option is going for 50¢, we could buy it back. What does this mean? We buy a $15 put for 50¢. Now we have the right to sell the stock at $15. The option costs $500 for ten contracts (plus commissions). You're now creating a "wash" situation. You sold 10 puts, now you've just bought 10 puts and to your broker's computer it's a wash. They both go off the screen. You now have no obligation to perform.

You would only buy back the puts if there were plenty of time before the expiration date for the stock to go back down. If the stock is near $15 and climbing, or above $15 with a small chance for a significant decrease, don't buy the put. Just wait for the option to expire and keep the whole $2,000. Your profit, if you buy back the $15 put for 50¢ ($500 for ten contracts) is $1,500. Don't unnecessarily spend money you don't have to. However, let's keep going. What if there is still plenty of time before the expiration date and the stock has shown a lot of volatility? It's at $15.50, the put options are 25¢, and you spend $250 to buy them back. You have a clear profit of $1,750, minus commissions. Now, the stock falls back to $14. At this time the $15 puts are going for $1.25. You sell another ten put contracts and generate $1,250, then one of the following happens.

1. The stock stays down. Your basis is now $12 ($15 minus $3: $2 for the original put sold, minus 25¢ for the put buy-back, plus $1.25 for the selling of the second $15 put). That is a super wholesale price.

2. The stock rises above $15. You get to keep the premiums and you have no further obligation.

3. If there is still time to buy back the put again, try it again—repeat the process. Note: I've done two puts, but never three in one month. It's possible, but highly unlikely. The stock would have to be really volatile, having a lot of quick movement. Look at the following charts and plays:

We sold puts at $15 and the stock went way up.

A good covered call stock can also be a good one for selling puts. We sold the $12.50 puts, then the stock hit $18. Profit $1,000.

We sold the $15 puts. We actually got the stock put to us, but I like this company and don't mind owning the stock.

DUCKS

Some of you have read elsewhere about DUCks—or Dipping Undervalued Calls. This is when a company's stock, usually after a split, which has been climbing, pulls back temporarily as investors take their profits. The company is solid and growing, but the stock dips 5 to 10% for no reason other than profit taking. Around our office we have a word for this. We call it a "sale." The price of the stock and also of the options has just dropped below value. It is a perfect buy opportunity.

Obviously, any buy opportunity or any rising stock also presents a great opportunity to sell a put. If the stock turns and rises (as it should) you keep the premium and that's it.

Of course, you want to pick the stock near the bottom of the dip and sell the put for the very next expiration date. And the strike price should be very near the stock price.

That way, if you're wrong and the stock gets put to you (you are required to buy it), you get it at the sale price where it can rise. When you buy a rising stock, you can easily sell later at a profit, sell calls, or just hold it. So a DUCk really presents a great opportunity to enhance your cash flow.

GOING SHORT

Up until now we have been discussing selling uncovered puts. We don't have a position in the underlying stock (as in writing covered calls). If you wanted to sell covered puts, you could, now or later, sell short the stock. You could generate cash, ride the stock on down, and when the stock falls in price (which is your risk in selling puts) you could cover your position by being short on the stock. If the stock gets put to you, it will cover (end) your short position.

Remember, you've agreed to buy stock you don't own. Now you've borrowed stock you don't own—you're covered. Sounds crazy, doesn't it?

Think of it this way. If you have to purchase the stock at $15, and your broker immediately sells 1,000 shares in a short sale, your obligation is covered. Now if there is a dip in the stock price, the stock you buy (at this lower wholesale price) will cover your short position.

This is a hedge. Now, let's double hedge. You hedge a short sale by purchasing call options. If the stock is at $13 and you still think there will be an increase, buy a $15 call option. Now you have the right to buy the stock at $15. The risk of short selling is an increase in the stock price. With the $15 call options, you've purchased insurance.

If the last several paragraphs frustrate you, read them again, discuss them with your broker, and don't worry too much. I've sold dozens and dozens of puts. I've only had to do short sales a couple of times. If you do your homework, and then sell the puts when the stock is way down and rising, you won't have to worry about this.

CASH REQUIREMENTS

The only true hang-up to selling puts is that your broker will require cash on hand (in-the-money market part of your account) to cover your obligation. If you have a margin account, you'll need to have around 30% of the amount needed to fulfill your obligation. If the stock is at $15, that's between $3,000 and $5,000. The money market account will earn interest. If you have a lot of money in your account, they will be a little more lenient. They just want to make sure you can take care of your obligation to purchase the shares if you have to buy them.

Other factors figure in, too. How many other stocks and options you own. How strong is your relationship? Each broker is different. Yes, they have strict SEC rules to follow, but they have their own concerns. The primary one being this: what is the exposure if there's a major market downturn–say 30%? Can you purchase all you've requested to purchase, or is their neck on the line too? They will err on the side of caution.

PROFIT AT SELLING PUTS (DAMAGE CONTROL)

You can't say that you have unlimited risk in selling puts because the lowest the stock can go is to zero. That is your downside. If the stock is below the strike price, it will get put to you.

You have one other strategy that can be played right up to and through the expiration date. It is called "rolling out." Here's the way it works. Let's say the stock is at $46. Last month you sold the $50 put for $2.25 when the stock was at $48.50. You had hopes it would go up. It hasn't. If you have to buy the stock, your basis will be $47.75 as you have received $2.25. One problem is the heavy-duty amount of cash you'll need to purchase the stock–even $25,000 on margin.

You think you could find a better use for the money. The put is currently $4.25–buy it back. Actually, you're just purchasing the same put (strike price, month) as you sold. This will close the position–it's a wash on your broker's computer. If you had ten contracts, you would have lost a little over $2,000 after you add up the commissions. You could just end it here, but don't. There's another play.

Remember, you liked this company's stock at this price. Check it out. Is the story line still in place? Yes, it didn't go above the $50 like you planned–at least, not yet. If you still think it will do so, roll on out to the next month.

Let's continue. Try to catch the stock on a dip–even if in a roll or slam in trading. Say it's going between $46⅝ and $46¾. It occasionally drops to $46¼. At that point, sell the November $50 put. It's going for $4.50. That's $4,500. You're back in the money again, and you've made a profit.

If you don't think it will go above $4.50, look at the $45 put. It's going for $2⅛, or $2.125. If you sold this you'd about break even on the original loss. Yes, you have an open position to buy the stock at $45, but your homework says it will go up.

Another method would be to split the contracts. Say, sell five of the $50 puts and five of the $45 puts. You should and could consider purchasing $45 or $50 calls. Maybe the $45s for November, and the $50s for February.

It keeps going down.

Believe me, there will be an end to this–you will eventually make money. The next month the stock is at $44. Let's stick with the $50 puts, as that will be most drastic. You sold the November 50 puts for $4.25. It will cost $6.50 to buy them back. This purchase will throw you back in the loss column. Not by much, though.

You're sure that this time the stock will turn around. It just has to (or so you hope). So spend the money–$6,500. Now the December $50 puts are going for $8 and the $45s are going for $2. Sell the $45 puts. You're profitable again. Also, look at the $40s–there might be some premiums there.

Now the stock moves back up to $47. Your December $45 put expires worthless, and you've made over $2,000 for all this trouble.

This could go on several months–but sometime (hopefully) the stock will turn around. When it does, you end it and keep the best batch of each. When you buy back this month's put you can always sell the next month out *for more money*.

AND FINALLY

There are two more considerations.

1. You may want to consider only selling, or at least primarily selling out-of-the-money puts, i.e. you sell the $50 put when the stock is at $52. This gives you a cushion. The problem is that the premiums are smaller and you have to weigh out the amount of margin tied up for the smaller option premium.

2. Stick with stocks in the $5 to $25 range. Selling puts and writing calls have a lot of the same risk/reward features–only in reverse. If you want nice premiums on stocks that won't kill you to buy, the lower priced stocks may work better.

Remember, when you sell you have many ways of making money (see "Tandem Plays"). When you buy call options or put options you only have one. This rolling out strategy lets you stay in the game until you make money.

It's simple: You generate cash whether you have to perform or not. If you do have to buy the stock, you purchased it at a less expensive price than otherwise. I love selling puts because you get the best of both worlds–cash now and wholesale prices.

11

OPTION EXIT STRATEGIES ON STOCK SPLITS

Many of my current strategies and much of my current profits are from trading options on companies announcing
stock splits. Exit strategies shown here are as varied as
entrance strategies. It would be appropriate to give additional sell plays
and do so in conjunction with the whole play (buy, hold, sell).

GETTING IN—GETTING OUT

PRE-ANNOUNCEMENT

I've had a lot of luck guessing which stocks are going to split. I look
at several things to see if the company may be ready to split.

1. Do they have a history of splits—and how recent are they? Value
    Line charts have information on splits. Other sources can be
    used.

2. Price range. Companies seem to split when they get near or
    above their previous high. Currently, I look for companies be-
    tween $120 and $280.

3. Profitability. Are they making money? Do they have growing
    revenues?

4. Dividends. Companies that pay dividends and announce larger dividends are good candidates for an increase in value. Companies that initiate dividends and do stock splits are great candidates.

5. Sympathy Moves. When other similar companies make stock split announcements, the hot potato passes on and can spread through a whole sector. Note: one week in early 1999, six major high-tech companies announced stock splits. Wed 1/21 Sun Microsystems (SUNW) 2:1, Sun also did another 2:1 in Dec 1999. Mon 1/26 Microsoft 2:1, Wed 1/28 Intel 2:1, Mon 1/26 IBM 2:1.

6. Companies that have stocks which run up in value in the previous six months—more specifically stocks with almost a 90% angle. Look at the following charts:

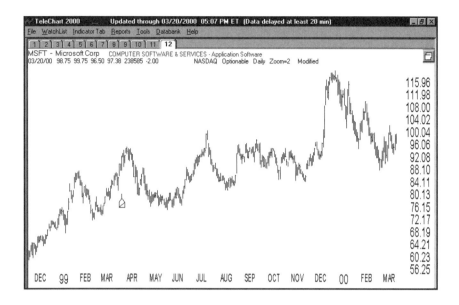

I want to make a special notation on Dell. Sometimes as companies announce a series of splits the float becomes huge. It incrementally becomes harder for the companies to reach their old high. Don't get me wrong: look at the profitability of purchasing 100 shares of Dell in 1996.

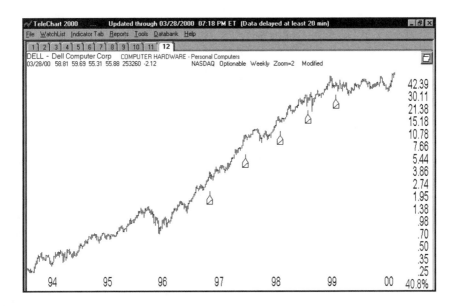

One hundred shares at $40 is $4,000. Then in June of '97 you have 200 shares at $50, now $10,000. After the next split in March, 1998 you would have 400 shares at $40, or $16,000. Another split in the summer of 1998 give you 800 at $50, or $40,000. One more split and you have in 1999, 1,600 at $50, or $80,000. Not bad for 2 ¹/₂ years.

However, look at the bar I've placed over the same chart. Do you see how the stock price did not rise back to the previous pre-split price—four times?

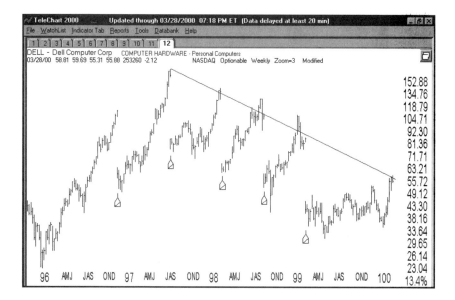

7. Find out when the board of directors meets, or when the annual shareholders' meeting is scheduled.

8. Check the information to be voted on at the shareholders' meeting and see if there is to be an authorization of new shares. Usually, but not always, this means a split is imminent (sometimes at the same meeting). For an example, observe Monsanto (MTC) in May of 1996.

Note: The directors usually don't need shareholder approval to do a stock split. However, they do need shareholder approval for new authorization of stocks because the shareholders numerical position will be diluted, hence the need for a vote. Check out Microsoft (MSFT) in the spring of 1994. They voted on more shares of stock. Shortly thereafter, they announced a 2:1 split scheduled to take place on May 23. Similar situations occur all the time, i.e. McDonalds (MCD) in May, 1996. Monsanto (MTC) voted on 140 million shares of additional authorized stock, then almost immediately announced a 5:1 split.

If you know exactly why you got in you should be able to choose the appropriate sell point.

I played another one called Zebra Technologies (ZBRA) that took almost six months, but it was still a good play.

The one that got my attention was Texas Instruments (TXN). It was near $140. I'm not making this up, but at 12:30 PM (PST–the stock market closes at 1:00 PM Pacific Time), I bought some $140 calls for the next month, and a few $145 calls two months out. At 1:15 PM, fifteen minutes after the market closed, the company announced a 2:1 split. They also increased their dividend. The stock shot up to $152 in the next few days and I got out at a huge profit.

You can't get lucky if you're not in the game.

Intuition? Maybe. Luck? Somewhat. But I do it all the time.

AFTER THE ANNOUNCEMENT

There is stock movement upon a stock split announcement and, for several days thereafter, there is usually a lot of volatility.

1. The period of time around the stock split–the day before, the day of, and the day after–has a lot of price fluctuations, usually positive in nature. Obviously, unless you pre-guess a split the day before it is announced, it comes and goes and you know nothing. Watch for quick run-ups, large volumes, et cetera–something is usually afoot.

> *On May 8th, during my second Wall Street Workshop™ (in*
> *San Diego), I bought 10 Cognos June $60 calls at $1¹/₈ on an-*
> *nouncement of a split. On May 14th, I sold them all at $16³/₄ for*
> *a profit of $6,927 and a return of 75.1%.*
>
> —R.L., CA

The day of the announcement is probably not a good time to play, which brings us to #2.

2. The day–actually the minute of the announcement–is a dangerous time. The problem is getting instantaneous information. If you have a news service or a broker with one (and one who will call you), and more specifically if he can do a word search on the word "split," then you can move quickly. Sometimes, the stock moves up $2 to $3 in a minute. Your $4 can become $6 in seconds. No joke, in seconds. We love having a stock split announcement occurring during one of our live Wall Street Workshops™. The attendees are amazed at how fast the options go up (and down). The problem is the options get so inflated. The stock could rise $3 and the option could go up $7 to $9. In a few days the "fluff" comes out of the premium and you're holding a losing option. Be careful not to purchase on "hype." Consider being a seller, not a buyer.

3. A day or so after the announcement. If there has been a huge increase there is a tendency for the stock (and therefore the option) to come back down. That's why I:

    a. Sell almost immediately–even if I lose some potential profits–and get out at a profit.

    b. Wait to see a better trend or better support. If the stock doesn't go up at first, I hold back and wait. This gives me time to really think about it, and wait for more news, earnings reports, dividends, et cetera.

4. On volatility: if the stock has been volatile before the split announcement, then it will probably continue to be volatile after the announcement and even after the actual stock split. If the company is a slow plodder–it will probably continue to be so.

The play is to buy on dips and sell at peaks. Remember: don't worry if you miss the first move. Be happy.

5. Before the actual split. Usually, the stock splits about four weeks after the announcement. Sometimes, it's six to ten weeks. Sometimes one week. Just before the split it may be a sale candidate. I've seen a lot of nice price increases during the short period before the actual split (exdividend date) and the day of the split. Then many stocks dip down. For example: an $80 stock runs up to $90 from the time of the announcement to the split date. The day before the split, it goes up to $92. It splits to two shares at $46. By the end of the day it's $47 and then a few days later it falls either to $44 or an $88 pre-split price. I've run across too many charts which show this pattern.

NETWORK SOLUTIONS (NSOL)
Network Solutions (NSOL) ran up $9 in one day just before the split before backing off and moving sideways after the split.

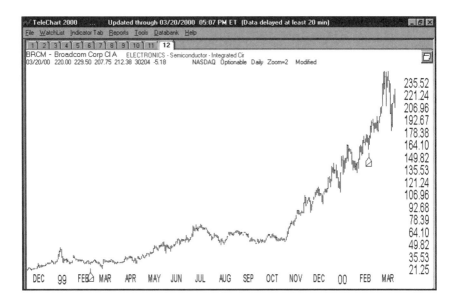

BROADCOM (BRCM)

Broadcom (BRCM) went from the $270 range to $338 in a matter of days just before it split. Once it split, it continued its upward trend for nearly a month before backing off.

YAHOO! (YHOO)

Yahoo! (YHOO) went from $300 to $360 in the weeks before the split, then backed off just before the split date.

DOUBLECLICK (DCLK)

Doubleclick (DCLK) moved from $200 to as high as $262 in the two days before the split, and then moved down for a couple of days. It then began a new rolling pattern.

EXODUS (EXDS)

Exodus (EXDS) moved strongly from $110 to $180 in the weeks before the split. It dipped slightly and then resumed a strong uptrend. As this is written, it is again back in split range, just three months later!

AMERICA ONLINE (AOL)

America Online (AOL) moved strongly into its split and then had a pull back after the split.

CNET (CNET)
CNET (CNET) split twice in the first half of 1999.

E-TRADE (EGRP)
E-Trade (EGRP) like CNET, this stock also split twice in early 1999.

CISCO SYSTEMS (CSCO)
As this was written, Cisco had just completed its second split in the last nine months.

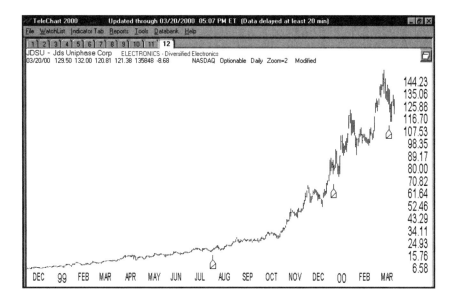

JDS UNIPHASE (JDSU)

In early March 2000, this stock completed its third split in only nine months.

I2 TECH (ITWO)

Another stock that was strong both before and after the split.

CITRIX SYSTEMS (CTXS)
This stock moved down a bit just before the split, and then continued its uptrend.

QUALCOMM (QCOM)
Qualcomm made one of the most incredible split runs ever, moving from about $200 to over $700 on the split date.

I can hardly ever find a stock that breaks this trend. I guess the quick pop-up cannot be sustained and it weakens once reality sets in. Investors start really examining it. (What is the stock really worth?) The euphoria is over; new news comes out, like lower projected earnings or similar news. Also, the time moves on to a "red light" period of time. See *Wall Street Money Machine, Volume 4: Safety 1ˢᵗ Investing.*

> *In August, 1998 I borrowed $30,000 on a credit card and bought 10 companies coming up to stock splits. The cost of borrowing the $30,000 was $500 monthly payments. In January 1999 my account was at $117,000. I paid off the $30,000 and had $87,000 left in my account less the $2,500 (5 months x $500 a month)! This was a net return of $84,500 on a $2,500 investment in just five months!*
>
> —MICHAEL F., MA

Also, here's a quick observation I've made. The stock (during and just after the split) moves, as do a lot of stocks, in sympathy with the market in general.

What does all this mean? If you're profitable you may want to exit just before (a day or hours) or just after the actual split. There will always be more time to buy back in. Yes, you might lose some potential profits, but this is more often the case: you purchase an option for $4, the stock was at $81. You own the $85 call. The company announced the split on July 2, and it is to take place August 19. You own the September 19 expiration date options. You've done it right. On August 8, the stock is at $87 and your option is $6, a nice 50% profit. On August 18, the stock shoots up to $90 and your option is worth $8—a double. On the 20th, the stock is at $46 ($92 pre-split) and your option is now $5.25. Should you sell or wait for it to go up more? On the 22nd, the stock dips $4 to $42 and your option (now the September $40 call) is $3. You are still profitable, but a lot less so. What if it dips further?

In this case, I would have sold. (I'm not just conjecturing here. I mean, not only would I have, I did sell at $5 or so.) I do this all the time. My people on W.I.N.™ wonder why I sell so quickly and so often.

Think about it. Wouldn't it be better to sell at $5.50, wait for a dip (even if it takes weeks or months) and buy back in at $3 (for the September) or even $4 for the October options? If the stock doesn't go down and there is more good news–if there is still plenty of time–buy back in at the October or November $45's or $50's.

You can get in and out many times along the way. You can buy the stock and wait it out, or you can buy the stock and sell. Proxy investing with options allows for a greater return and many short-term profits. You have less cash tied up and you can jack up your profits by being nimble and quick.

12

TANDEM PLAYS

This chapter is about winning–and winning big. No time for mediocrity and no time for second best. My continued drive as an educator is to consistently find new, better, faster ways to make money. I love a barbecue (BBQ). To me it stands for Bigger, Better, and Quicker returns. In dealing in the stock market this means returns, yields–money back in. In short, more INcome–INfaster, INbigger quantities, and INmore often.

I'm not alone in this endeavor. My students, countrywide, share ideas, hints, and techniques that have helped them make more. I've become a clearinghouse of ideas–some boring, some not too hot, but many are great ways to enhance our earning potential. For years, I've said I want to help people get their money working as hard as they work. Now, after two decades as an educator, I realize why people had a quizzical look when I said that. They actually want their money to work *harder* than they do. I also realize one other thing: you've all heard the one about working smarter, not harder; well, the real-life application of that is to improve upon those investors who are "true doers," who really think about what they're doing–who can and do improve upon their methods, their results, and their applications.

If you like to deal in stock options, these new ideas–actually varia-tions of how we look at and use old ideas, will help you see new av-enues, fortify your resolve for perpetual and consistent income, and actually help you generate more cash flow.

This is a tough order for some of you, because you're doing so well. Others need this information to get off dead center. Maybe by explaining option alternatives this will be accomplished.

However, no matter who you are or why you're reading this, you should have read other reports or books (hopefully written by Yours Truly) on option investing. You should be familiar with calls and puts. If not, stop now and go back to the basics.

WIN MORE THAN YOU LOSE

I've repeatedly said that two things make stock market trading prof-itable:

1. Be right more than you are wrong.

2. Be willing and able to act quickly. If you haven't figured out by now that options move extremely fast and big when the un-derlying stock moves even a little, then there may be no hope for you. It's not this aspect that I want to deal with. It's the first point–being right more often–that I'll write about. You've heard the one about Babe Ruth striking out more than 3,000 times on his way to the home run record, so I won't bring it up here. And even if I did, that's only part of the point I'm about to make. I want to help you stack the deck in your favor.

So, after all this set up, let me just say the main point–the theme of this chapter. Then I will explore it, dissect it and put it to work.

Here it is:

When you sell calls or sell puts you have a two out of three chance of making money.

The deck is stacked in your favor. I'll follow up with diagrams and explanations, but first let's look at the four plays.

All of these deal with options—a derivative based on an underlying stock. I like stock options because they are not a pure gamble (as are index options, currency options and interest rate options) and you actually can buy or sell the underlying stock.

Let's quickly review the basics. A call option is the right to buy a stock. You can buy call options and you can sell call options. A put option is the right to sell a stock. You can buy put options and you can sell put options.

BUY	STOCK PRICE	SELL
Call	Rises	Call
	Steady	
Put	Falls	Put

Look at the diagram closely because we're going to explore variations of these options.

Let's explain this further and then see how you win two out of three times—and maybe every time if you do it right.

WHY AND WHEN
BUYING CALLS

You buy calls (short and long term) when you think a stock (hence the option value) will increase within a certain time period. You do so to lock in a certain price for the stock or to sell the option at a higher price. Your risk is that the stock (option) won't increase in value in the time allowed.

SELLING CALLS

You sell calls to generate income. When you sell a call, you are committed to perform. You've given someone the right to buy stock from you, whether you own (covered) the stock or not (uncovered, naked). The premium you receive adjusts the basis you pay (paid) for the stock. For example, if you bought a stock at $9 and sold the $10 strike price call for $1 and then had the stock bought from you at $10, your profit would be $2. Your basis is $8, as the $1 premium reduces your basis from $9 to $8.

You can systematically generate monthly income from writing (sell-ing) calls. You sell naked call options when stocks are high and you expect them to go down or stay the same. (See the chapters on cov-ered calls in *Wall Street Money Machine, Volume 1.*)

I have what I feel is a great "buying put" story. Following in the great tradition of Wade Cook's Wall Street Money Machine, *I purchased 20 contracts of a put on LSI Logic Corp. (LSI) at $2^{13}/_{16} on July 2, at a $25 strike with an October expiration date. I also did a call strategy on this stock as well.*

This stock then became fairly stagnant and I almost sold my put yesterday (July 9) for not much profit, but I held on one more day and on Wednesday, July 10th, I was able to sell my put for $4^5/_8. This gives me a profit of approximately $3,625.

—T.H., KY

Again, you can write covered calls and uncovered calls. If you write uncovered calls you may get a great rate of return, as you about 30 to 50% of the stock price tied up in margin. You also have an added risk in that you may have to purchase the stock for resale if the stock rises above the strike price and you get called out. Obviously, this risk is mitigated by the premium you've received. For example: if you've sold a call (when the stock was at $11) for a $2 premium at a $10 strike price, you'd hope for the stock to go below $10. You'd only sell the call if you thought the stock would go, or stay, under the strike price, so you could keep the premium with no further obligation. For other varia-tions, attend the Wall Street Workshop.

I nearly paid for the cost of the course with three days of investing! I know you at [Stock Market Institute of Learning] will believe it, but I'm sure others will not. Thanks for the best business course I have ever taken. I highly recommend the Wall Street Workshop™ to anyone who is interested in financial stabil-ity. Sounds crazy to accomplish this in stocks. Just test it! Knowl-

edge is the key to the stock market. Thank you for providing the
information I needed.

-R. T., CA

I really like to sell uncovered calls. It takes experience and more
cash in your account to do these, but it's fun and very profitable. I also
employ bear call spreads (see *Wall Street Money Machine, Volume 4*).

BUYING PUTS

Now, let's get on to puts. The right (option) to sell a stock to someone increases in value as the stock moves downward and away from
the strike price. If the stock is $38 and you think it will go down, you
could buy a put option with a $30, $35, $40 or $45 strike price. The
one you choose depends on:

1. How far down you think the stock will go.

2. How much you want to risk (your option premium).

3. How much time before the expiration date.

4. Other important factors:

    a. whether the stock rolls between certain ranges

    b. news regarding debt, mergers, new (good, bad) manage-
        ment, et cetera.

A $2.50 premium to buy a $40 put will increase in value as the
stock moves to $36, $35 and lower. You can sell or exercise the option
any time before the expiration date.

SELLING PUTS

If you sell a put, everything turns upside down. You are selling the
right to someone to put the stock to you at the strike price. Why do
this?

1. To generate immediate income. Think of it. If the stock goes
    above the strike price you won't get it put to you and you get
    to keep all of the premium.

2. You buy the stock wholesale. Let's say the stock is at $13 and
    you sell the $15 put for $2.50, the stock doesn't rise above $15

(maybe it is $14.50) and you get it put to you, your basis is $12.50. You've just bought a $14.50 stock for $12.50.

When do you do this?

1. When you want to own stock in a company, or, at least, you wouldn't mind owning it.

2. When you wouldn't mind owning it at that price–and wholesale, to boot.

3. You want to generate income–*now*!!

CROSSOVER

Now that we've established the four plays, look at the following diagram.

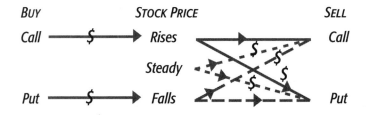

There are three things that can happen to the stock (and we assume this movement will affect the option price to a certain degree): it can stay the same or about the same, it can go up, and it can go down. However, if you sell a call or a put, a lot of opportunities open up. You should see here that you could sell a put in the situation where you normally would think of buying the call (you think the stock is going to rise) and sell a call when you would buy a put (you think the stock will fall). The difference and the key point is that when you sell something you generate income.

So, if you think a stock is going up, you can sell a put rather than buy a call to place dollars into your account instead of spending it. That's cash flow: selling rather than buying. If you 1) buy back the option you sold at a lower price, or 2) let the option expire, you get a great rate of return. By selling options, two out of the three possible scenarios (stock rises, stock stays steady, or stock falls) are profitable.

When you buy options the stock must move one way. Only one profitable scenario exists. Look at the following examples:

SELLING CALLS

The stock is, say $9, and you write the $10 call and receive $1.50 premium. If the stock rises above the strike price and you are called out, you keep the premium, but you have to deliver the stock.

If the stock stays steady at $9 or falls below $9, you can either buy back the call at a lower price when the time value decays, or you could wait for the option to expire. In either case, you would receive a nice rate of return.

SELLING PUTS

The stock is, say $11, and you write the $10 put and a $1.50 premium. If the stock stays the same or rises, you keep the premium and you can either buy back the put at a lower premium or wait for the option to expire. Either way, you get a nice return.

If the stock falls below the strike price of $10, you have the stock put to you. You would have to accept the stock at $10.

COVERED CALLS

If you purchased the stock at $9 and wrote the $10 call for $1.50, you would receive a $1.50 premium. If the stock rises above the strike price ($10), you would be called out, and you would keep the $1.50 premium plus make $1 on the sale of the stock.

If the stock stays steady, you would not be called out. You would keep your $1.50 premium and you could write more calls the next month.

If the stock falls, you keep the $1.50 premium which can offset the loss on your stock. Then you have to make a choice, do you wait for expiration or buy back the call at a reduced price?

COVERED PUTS

Covered puts are an odd concept to explain. In a covered call, you own the stock, so you can deliver it if the option is exercised against you. In a covered put, you have to have a place in your portfolio prepared and ready to accept stock if it is put to you, i.e. you must have a short sale position in that stock.

> *I like selling puts on a stock that I would like to own in a long-term position even through market turmoil. By selling a pricey put, you can take advantage of the speed of options and, if it all goes well, you can buy it back at a profit. If it doesn't all go as planned and it gets put to you, you will just own a stock you wanted anyway. You can start selling covered calls at the strike price you paid (after adjusting for the premium collected) for the stock when the stock has regained strength before a dip. Then, when it dips, you buy the call back. Continue to sell these perhaps deep-in-the-money calls until you get called out.*

> *I have been doing this with Ascend Communications (ASND). It seems to work well because it is such a great stock for this strategy. This strategy could be disaster for someone who tried this with Micron Technology (MU) a while back. Perhaps buying some cheap puts at the same time may work as a safety hedge. Options can be risky this year. I find that buying options when the McClellan Oscillator is in an oversold condition can help me not get stung by a correction or market rotation. Keeping track of future event dates like jobs reports can be helpful, too. The bad thing is that one can wait a long time between these safer trading periods. A strong, long-term, up-trending stock can make a big difference.*

> —A. L., CA

STOCK LOW—GOING UP (SELL PUT—BUY CALL)

If you sold the put for $2.50 ($2,500) and bought the call for 25¢ ($250), you would have a net in of $2,250. Now, as the stock increases, you can either buy back the put or just let it expire (in most cases). The call could now be sold for $1.50 or $1.75, generating more income.

STOCK PRICE	PUT PRICE ($15.00)	CALL PRICE ($15.00)
$13.00	$2.50	$0.25
13.50	1.75	0.50
14.00	1.25	1.00
14.50	0.50	1.25
14.75	0.25	1.50
15.50	0.13	1.75

You get rich (cash flow rich) by selling–get better at getting out than at getting in.

If you have to get in, do so at wholesale prices.

If you have to get out, do so at retail prices.

STOCK PRICE	CALL PRICE	PUT PRICE
$15.75	$1.50	$0.25
15.00	1.00	0.75
14.50	0.75	1.00
14.00	0.50	1.25
13.50	0.43	1.50
13.00	0.125	2.25

STOCK HIGH–COMING DOWN (SELL CALL–BUY PUT)

Sell the call for $1.50 ($1,500 if you purchased ten contracts) buy the put for 25¢. Capitalize on each–depending on the time left before expiration–at the optimum time. Buy back the call or let it expire and sell the put at a profit.

You know I like getting rich in bite-sized pieces–Two plays on the same movement–talk about two mints in one!

Once again, so many more opportunities open up when you sell than when you buy. Don't misunderstand; I still make most of my money buying calls–on pure option plays. I try, however, to sell as many calls and puts as I can. Remember, writing covered calls is a great strategy for IRA's and other pension-type accounts.

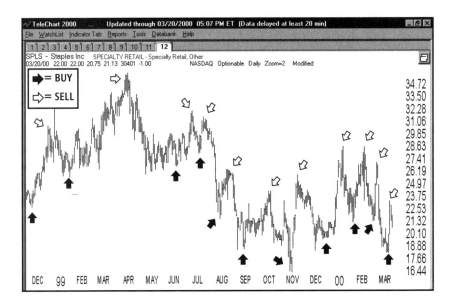

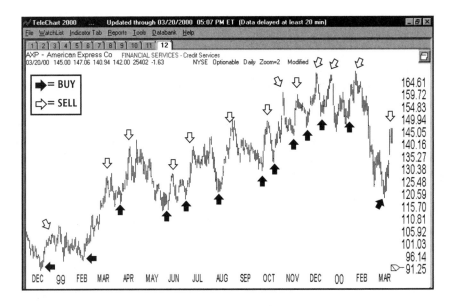

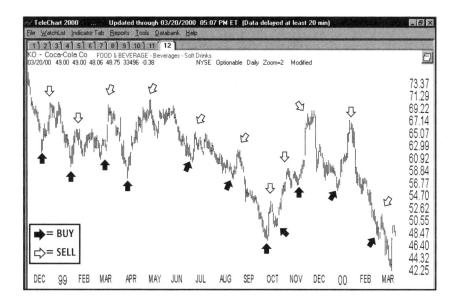

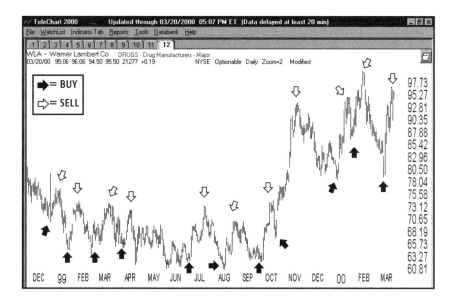

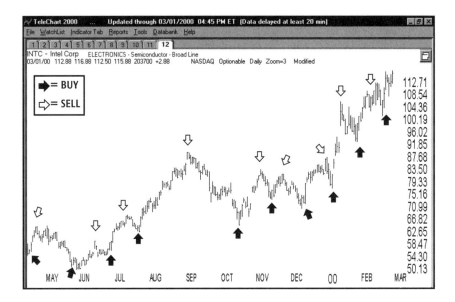

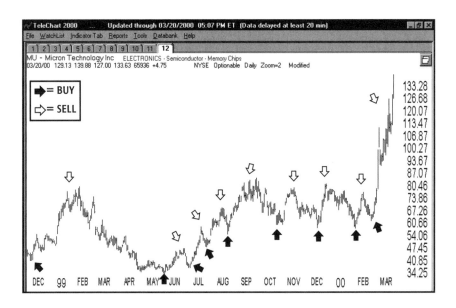

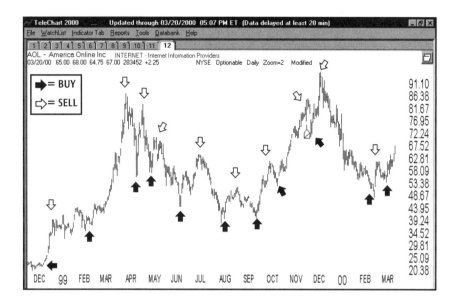

Generating income, infinite returns, buying stock wholesale, double-dipping with highly volatile stocks (selling two calls or puts in one month)–are just so much fun.

Now look at the following charts to see possibilities. I added arrows to show the buy and sell ranges.

Read the following example: you find a stock that is rolling, rising from $13 and bouncing off $16. It's down to $13 and is rising quite rapidly. When it hits $13.50, you sell the $15 put for $2. Ten contracts equal $2,000. Nice cash flow.

Now, when the stock gets to $14.75, the put is going for 50¢. You buy it back at a cost of $500. You get to keep the $1,500 with no further obligation. However, why not cross over and sell the $15 call? Do this when the stock is at $15.50 or $15.75. Yes, it might rise or stay above $15 and you'd have to buy the option back at a small loss, but the $15 premium could easily be $1 to $1.50–another $1,500 of income. Remember to check the charts. This one is moving rapidly. It may go under $15 and you'll have a second premium–yours to keep. Now as it dips down and starts up, repeat the process.

True, when it's above $15 and you think it's going down you could do a pure $15 put purchase play. And yes, when it hits $12 or $13 you could do a pure $12.50 call, or $15 call purchase play.

You could even do a double play.

1. Sell a $12.50 put and buy a call when the stock is at $13 when you believe it's on the way up. The premium will be about the same. However, as the stock rises, the money you received for selling the put looks better because the put value goes down (remember, you sold it when it was nice and high). At the same time your call premium goes up in value. Sell the call now for a profit and keep the profit for selling the put, or even buy back the put while it's low. Wow, I can't wait for the market to open tomorrow. And yes, we can wax philosophical all day long–hey, if I have to potentially buy the stock at $15 and I've purchased the right to buy it at $15, what if it's close? Your brain might catch on fire.

2. Sell a call and buy a put when you think a stock may go down
    a bit. This way you pick up the nice call premium. If you own
    the stock, you won't get called out. The dip is offset by the rise
    in value of the put option premium. You can sell the put option
    at a profit.

    If you don't own the stock, you keep the premium for selling
    the call and then get to sell the put at a higher price when the
    stock goes down. This is a form of hedging, and what a hedge
    it is!

Now, don't make this too complicated. You've read about rolling
stocks and rolling options. You've heard me teach about peaks and
valleys. You've heard of some straddles–buy a call and put on the same
stock, same month, same strike prices, and wait for a big move either
way. Well, I call this a side-straddle. A calculated, predictable way to
capture the up movement, or the down movement–*twice*.

I cover this more extensively at the Wall Street Workshop™. You'd
be smart to be there. Call 1-800-872-7411. These seminars sell out, so
call now.

1

BEHIND CLOSED DOORS

Publisher's note: The following was taken from a training session by Wade Cook with Robert Hondel, the General Sales Manager for Stock Market Institute of Learning™ and a group of new sales people. This is an actual training session by Wade Cook. What is remarkable about this session is that Wade doesn't teach sales techniques; he simply teaches about our products and what they can do for people. We thought you as a customer would like to read this.

Hello, this is Wade Cook. This is going to be a training session because I feel that there's a real strong need for our new sales people, and possibly some of our older sales people, to have my verbal statements in regard to marketing and selling our Wall Street Workshop™. Let me tell you where this came from, then I'm going to give you a brief history about me and the company in just a second.

We have such an incredible product. I know that that word is used so much today, but the Wall Street Workshop™ really is a seminar workshop that makes a difference in a lot of people's lives. I don't think any of you in our new sales department would be here if you did not also believe that.

Maybe you've come to work for us after going through our seminar. We have a lot of people who were students before. Or maybe you have a friend that's working here now. I'll be very honest with you, I was a little bit dismayed several weeks ago when I was doing a training session and just out of the blue thought, "I'm going to test everybody on this." So I had everybody pull out a blank piece of paper and write on it five reasons why anybody should come and attend the Wall Street Workshop™. I gave them five or 10 minutes and then, one by one, I started gathering them up.

The comments were all correct, but they were boring. I started thinking, "My goodness, I wonder if our sales people are saying these things on the phone." I'll just give you a couple of examples right now, and I will deal with more later on.

"You can start making money right away."

"You gain control over your retirement income."

To me these are true and they could be exciting to certain people, but they're too bland. There's not enough adjectives or adverbs in there. They don't explain and really tell what we do, and obviously there is no emotion behind these at all. Because of this lack of emotion, I decided to come into the studio to take some of these sentences, rework them, put some meat on the bones, and make them exciting. When people are calling in on the phone, I contend that they are not calling to be bored. They're calling in for a reason. We need to figure out that reason and give them a non-boring answer. So, I'm going to go through several of these statements and help you assist the people on the phone understand what the Wall Street Workshop™ is all about, and what it can mean in their lives.

First, I'm going to give you a brief history. I know there are a lot of new people here, and maybe you've seen some of my real estate books. I got my start in the investment arena in real estate. I was a cab driver in Tacoma, Washington, and I learned that the secret to making money was in the Meter Drop™. It wasn't in trying to make a killing on any one deal. It was making a killing on a whole bunch of small deals, getting the taxi moving for $3 to $6 runs, instead of waiting for the $35 to $50 runs to SeaTac airport.

I've been in the investment business now over two decades, but in the teaching part of it about, almost 18 years. I guess I didn't learn my lesson very well, because I was very successful at real estate investing and I was very successful at the seminar business: teaching people, writing books, et cetera. However, back then I wasn't very good at the stock market. I didn't realize that I could take strategies that I had learned in the taxi and in real estate–the Meter Drop™, buying and selling, doing as many small deals as I possibly could do–and use those same strategies in the stock market. However, I ended up by doing just that. It is a process I call "rolling stock," but some stockbrokers call it "channeling." It rolls up, and it rolls down. Then I discovered "writing covered calls," and later I developed my stock split strategies.

I want to make a lot of money. I want to lead the way, and then show people how they, too, can make a lot of money and really make a difference in their lives. When I say, "Make a lot of money," I don't mean just $9,000 or $10,000 on one deal. I mean start with $5,000 or $6,000 and learn how to make $8,000 or $9,000 a month, every month. These are the concepts we teach at the Wall Street Workshop™.

I'm going to go through several things about the Wall Street Workshop™ in answer to the people's questions. The first thing you've got to ask yourself is, "Why are they on the phone? Why are they calling?" Now, they may have heard me on a radio show, or they may have heard me during a PR tour for my book, *Wall Street Money Machine, Volume 1*. Now we're coming out with *Volume 2, Stock Market Miracles*, and soon, *Volume 3, Bulls & Bears*. When these books hit, it gets our phones ringing. People call up and say, "Well, what is this training, this Wall Street Workshop™? What is this Next Step™ seminar?"

Remember, every sale is an emotional sale. Let me say that again. Every sale is an emotional sale. People are buying our products to fulfill a need. If they don't know how to do stock market investing very well, then they can come to the Wall Street Workshop™. In an immersion learning format, they will spend two days doing deals, getting involved, and seeing the 13 different cash-flow strategies. We tell people what to do at the Wall Street Workshop™, show them how to do it, and then we watch over them while they do it. If they have their mobile phones, they go to the side of the room, out in the hallway, or on a hotel lobby phone, and call their stockbrokers. Whether they do the deal or not, we want them to go call, get quotes, and start figuring these things out for themselves.

Then they can come back into the seminar. If they actually bought an option or a stock, we can talk about it, discuss it, and go over the formula. We want people to see these deals done because experiential learning is the best way. We all know that. It's on-the-job training. I want you to think about that. Even here in the sales department when you're a brand new sales person, we put you with our more experienced sales people so you can see how they work with people, how they explain things to people. That's on-the-job training. Why should things of a financial nature be any different?

The irony is that a lot of our people who come through the Wall Street Workshop™ end up making, within a month or two, what their business is making. So they may spend a whole month working 40 to 60 hours a week running their business and make $8,000, $9,000. Then they start with $2,000 or $5,000 in the stock market and after they learn the Wade Cook strategies, they start making $5,000 to $8,000 a month. That's per month! And they're only working 15 minutes a day, two or three days a week. It's a whole world of difference. That's what we're trying to show people at the Wall Street Workshop™.

I keep stating that I'm in the retirement business. We want to help people get retired. Now, there are many, many roads that people can take. You may need to ask and find out before you get too far involved in the explaining process about the Wall Street Workshop™, why did they call? Where is their major area of concern? Where do they have a lot of their investments now? Are they in real estate? Do they have their own businesses? Are they working at a job for someone else? If they have stock market investments, is it primarily mutual funds? Et cetera, et cetera, et cetera. You need to know, because there are many roads to getting wealthy. I think that we have a great, great course, but we're just one of a lot of different types of seminars. However, nobody at all (that I know of) is teaching the experiential learning formatted seminar where you come, learn, and do the deals.

Remember that you're all my ambassadors for Stock Market Institute of Learning™. An entity I manage, personally owns the copyright to Wall Street Workshop™. It has licensed with Stock Market Institute of Learning™, the seminar corporation under our publicly traded company called Wade Cook Financial Corporation, to market the Wall Street Workshop™. The instructors are hand-trained by me.

Let's go back to people on the phone. When they call, they're looking for something to help them make money. They're looking at our company's products to see if they will take them where they want to go. It's like they're sitting at a train stop. A train comes through and they look at all the markings on it. They think, "Is this one going to go where I want it to go?" That one leaves, another train comes, and they question if it's the right one. At some point in time, they're going to see us. Hopefully they will say, "Wow, this train is on the right track. This train is going where I want it to go."

If something goes wrong, for example we have a recession or a down market, here's the train that's going to help me through that. People will need us more during those times. There are so many people talking about a bear market, and in the long run, who cares about bear markets anyway? They only last nine to twelve months, and there are three bull markets for every bear market. The average bull market–where stocks have increasing price ranges–lasts three to five years. The average bear market lasts about nine months. Why would anybody dedicate their lives to serving the bear? That's why I wrote this book coming out called *Wall Street Money Machine, Volume 3: Bulls & Bears* (formerly titled *Bear Market Baloney*). There are so many things that people can do if there is a bear market. Money can be made in a down market, just not quite as easily as an up market. We encourage people not to get caught up in the negative.

We're discussing people looking at us. They say, "Is this train, this vehicle going where I want it to go? And if something breaks down, are there people that will fix it? Can they really help me?" Now, what I try to do at our seminars, not only the stock market seminars, but all of our asset protection and tax seminars, is to make sure that we give the best financial education in this country. We have the Wealth Institute™, our incredible flagship, three-day course. We have our B.E.S.T. (Business Entity Skills Training) seminars. We have additional real estate and other kinds of stock market seminars. We have a whole division of our company that sets up legal entities: Nevada Corporations, Charitable Remainder Trusts, Family Limited Partnerships, and many more.

Our company really is about five things: 1) we want to show people how to make money. This translates into three categories: real estate, the stock market, and small business. 2) we want to show people how to lower their exposure to risk and liability. 3) we want to show people how to eliminate, or at least reduce, but possibly eliminate their taxes. 4) help them prepare for a great retirement. And 5) we call bequeathment: making sure that somebody–their friends, family, or church–in a tender, loving, caring way, gets everything that they worked so hard to build up. We have all the notes to play the chord. Some people who come through our training are going to hear the symphony.

It's really important to me that before any of your clients come to the Wall Street Workshop™ that you help them prepare for it. This is not an experiential class for experienced people in the stock market. It is also not just a beginners' class. We want people to know the vocabulary, we want people to know certain words. So, here's a couple of things that they should do.

Before they come to the class, they should definitely read *Wall Street Money Machine, Volume 1*, hopefully once, but maybe even twice. They should get the *Zero to Zillions*™ home study course, which from time to time we have for free as a bonus if they sign up for the Wall Street Workshop™. Another thing they can do before they come is to paper trade. We have a book called *On Track Investing* by Dave Hebert that is all about simulation trading. If they're afraid of investing their own money, say $5,000 cash, why not take $5,000 and fictitiously invest it? Buy and sell, buy and sell.

Definitely people need to get on W.I.N.™, which is our Wealth Information Network™. It's on the Internet at www.wadecook.com. People can access it, go in, and find out what trades and strategies we are actually doing that day. They can see trades being made.

We get in testimonials all day long. Here's a lady that says, "I made $763 within 30 minutes. If I'm called out, I will make over $1,000." That's a covered call.

Sandi from New Jersey said, "Cash flow is the way of making money. I netted $2,100 in two days. The Wall Street Workshop™ is the best financial seminar I've ever attended."

Listen to what Wayne said from Florida, "In two days and one covered call, I made $1,875. If I get called out I will get another $630, for a total of $2,505." I can hardly read all of these testimonials anymore. They just keep pouring in.

All right, let's get to some of these quotes. Here we go. These are the statements that I collected several weeks ago when I asked all the existing sales people to make a list of the reasons why people should come to the Wall Street Workshop™. Here's what they said.

"The education you receive is taught nowhere else." Well, that's an understatement. What we teach are formulas, strategies, and techniques. I'm not that concerned about a particular stock or mutual fund. We go out and find a stock that fits our formula. Whether it's rolling stock, covered calls, options on stock splits, or selling puts, people need to learn these really neat strategies. They become the tools, if you will, in our students' tool chest. Once they have the tools in their tool chest, they can go fix a Ford, a Chevy, or a Chrysler, but they've got to have the tools. We get people the tools. Nobody even comes close to teaching the types of strategies that we do. Do you know why? Because most people, including stockbrokers, do not even know they exist.

The next comment by one of our sales people was, "You receive real value for your money because it is an experiential seminar, not just another lecture." Now, that's what I've been harping on all along–real value. People want value. When they spend 79¢ on an ice cream cone, or $18,000 on a car, what they want is to make sure what they spend is coming back in the form of value. So much value that they can say, "I got a good deal." Well, that's exactly what we want people to say. When they get out of the Wall Street Workshop™, we want them saying, "Man, that was a great experience."

Now, I must tell you right up front that if we ever get complaints about the Wall Street Workshop™ (which we hardly ever do) it's from people who did not do the trades. I've only had a few people who have said something like, "Well, we didn't do enough trades." When I go talk to the speaker they may say, "Well, we did 23 trades in class." Then, I always come back and ask, "What trades did you make?" If I ever get a complaint, and they are very, very seldom, it usually comes from people who aren't doing any deals. I learned a long time ago that producers produce, nonproducers complain.

People want value for their money and we want to make sure that when they get done with our seminar, it is one of the best values they have ever receive.

Okay, the next one says, "You could start making money right away." Well, no kidding. Right in class, people jump up when we're doing a Monsanto 5:1 stock split or a Boeing stock split, or whatever, and call their stockbrokers. They make money. Then three hours later they sell out. They spend $5 on 10 contracts, that's $5,000, and they sell them for $7, which is $7,000, a $2,000 profit within two or three hours, or maybe the next day. Usually, though, within a week or two of the class, most people have made the tuition of the class back easily, but sometimes three, four, and five times the amount of money they invested to come.

Think about this. If you can come to a course and learn how to make $3,000 or $4,000 in one day, then, how much can you make, and how many more two-day segments are there for the rest of the year? A hundred of them? Well, a hundred at $2,000 is $200,000 for the year. That is not an impossible income. Yes, they can start making money right away. We need to realize that the burden of teaching and show-ing the formulas and techniques is on us, but the burden of doing the deals is on the student.

The next comment that a salesman made was, "You gain control over your retirement income." I think everybody wants that. Every-body wants more income. Think about it. Your need for tax write-offs is going to change from year to year. Anybody's need for growth is going to change and get more as they get older. But, your need for income will always change, and it will always change in that you need more. As you retire, you need more money. You know what? 90% of all Americans have to substantially cut down their standard of living upon retirement. Well, we want to change that. We want to make people get to the point where they can retire, raise their standard of living, have more money coming in, and be able to do so with as little time as possible spent managing their money.

The next comment was, "The package includes a home study course." From time to time it does, sometimes with the tuition or W.I.N.™. My comment here is that they can keep learning and refresh their memory. Repetition and duplication are the best teacher. We want to not only expose them to these ideas and strategies once for the two days, but to have them continually learning more. That's why we have such a discount on coming back and taking the Wall Street Workshop™ a second time. So, don't forget to tell people that there's a retake price, which is very, very reasonable.

The next comment a salesman said was, "It is a three step seminar: first teaching, then showing, and finally doing the deals." Now, that's a great one that I can't say any better. It is an experiential learning formatted seminar. I keep saying that and I don't know if anybody that calls in can really understand. People come to the seminar and do deals right in class. They make money now, not later. That is what makes us different. That's experiential learning.

The next comment was, "It's an exciting life changing event that will permanently alter your lifestyle." That's a great comment. That sounds a little bit nebulous though. From my experience in the educational field, every time you use the words "life changing," I don't see a lot of people that want to change. If they do say they want to change, what they really want is everybody else around them to change. They want their stockbrokers to find all the good deals, they want everybody out there to find the good deals for them.

What we're going to help people do, hopefully, is overcome fear with knowledge. We're going to help them overcome fear by actually doing the deals. Why not come to class and do the deals in class so that when you get home, you hit the ground running? That's the point.

Yes, it is an exciting, life changing event. It's like a real epiphany to some people to literally come, call their stockbrokers, see deals being made, and actually make money. For the first time in their life, they've been able to take $3,000 and in a matter of hours, make that $3,000 into $5,000. That's a $2,000 profit. Tell me if that doesn't change your lifestyle. Or change your life.

The next one says, "The Wall Street Workshop™ enhances the learning curve in stock market investing to increase your profits." Well, that's what it's all about. Let me tell you the name of the game. The name of the game is, "teach me the rules and I'll play your game."

What we're trying to do is get people through this learning process as quickly as they possible can. We start slow and then explain certain things, but as soon as we can, we're into the deals. I want to make sure that all of my sales people know that the instructors are not only trading in their own accounts, but we have every instructor signed onto our major instructors' accounts with the company.

The next comment was, "We'll show you hands on work, so you can do it yourself with the 13 strategies we teach." I want to be careful with the word "hands on" here. A lot of people think that they're going to come and somebody's going to literally take them by the hand, walk out there, and call their stockbroker with them. We're not in the babysitting business. We teach the correct principles, and people govern themselves. Our "hands on" means that they're going to see the deals being done. Again, it's the experiential learning format.

The next comment was, "The Wall Street Workshop™ is worth 50 times the amount you pay because of the value you receive from what you learn." I agree. I don't think there's any way to say 50 times, or 100 times because it might cost you $3,000 or $4,000 for a course that shows you how to make $200,000 a year. What does it cost? I've said a lot in my seminars, "It will cost people. This is the first time anybody has ever put together a seminar that will cost a lot more to stay home than it will to attend." I don't know how much your average students are making, but I've got so many letters about people who are making $100,000 to $200,000 a year, after starting with $5,000 or $10,000. Well, what did it cost them?

The next comment was, "Wade's strategies increase your confidence in trading and decrease your risk of loss." That's exactly what they do. You learn the strategy that has the bear market behind everything we do, the desire to not lose money. Yes, they're brand new, they're not brand new in terms of being around the stock market, we have just taken existing strategies and have put them to work on a continued basis. If there's any genius that I have, it is being persistent and consistent with something that works.

I am reminded of a story of Woody Hayes, the famous football coach. He had a great halfback, but he kept getting tackled. Time after time after time, he would just run right into a wall and get tackled. Finally the coach called the young boy over to the sidelines and said,

"Boy, run where they ain't." That's kind of what I've done. I want to run where they ain't. I want to do things that other people don't even know how to do, to show people how they, too, can make more money.

The next comment by a salesman says, "You can network with those around you to continue to learn from each other." That's an important point. Rubbing shoulders with people who are trying to do better and be better can teach you a lot.

The next one is, "Your financial outlook will change forever." Boy, how do we quantify that? Somebody's financial outlook? Yes, I agree. Once you learn how to make money, you will never go back. Once your brain has expanded, it will never go back to its original dimensions.

We talk about an outlook. For some people, it's like cleaning off a dirty window. You can't believe how many people have come who've now quit their jobs, or one spouse has quit and they're at home taking care of the kids instead of them being at a day care center. They're there loving their kids, working 10 to 20 minutes a day, in their pajamas, calling their stockbrokers, and making money.

The next comment that people made is really important. I don't know who said this one, but it says, "This can enhance or replace your current income." Isn't that what people want? If people want to wind down their business or quit their job, what is the one thing they need to replace? They don't need to replace the busyness of it. They need to replace the income. I really believe this country needs three things. Number one is parents spending more time with their kids. And number two, see number one. Number three, see number one. If there's anything I can do, or my staff can do, to help people be a better mother or father, it is to spend more time with their kids. You can even involve your family in parts of this dynasty building. Then it becomes wonderful. But, in order to quit the job to be at home, what do you need? You need income. That's what this seminar is about, building up income.

The next one says, "It's exciting group participation." That's true, because you learn a lot by being around other people. You can learn a lot on your own, but what if there were another 150 people in class, and you're assigned to a team of 10 to 15 people, and you're all making money. You all bounce ideas off each other and catch each others' enthusiasm.

This next one says, "It's an opportunity to do what you learn, while learning." That's kind of interesting. Let me say that in another way. People can earn while they learn. They can earn money while they are sitting there learning. If they learn it well and learn how to apply these principles, they can continually learn earning money over and over again. In this experiential learning format, they can earn while they learn. I'm going to come back to several more like this, but I want to talk to you a little bit about a few other things.

While being honored at a New York banquet, Albert Einstein told a young hostess, "I'm engaged in the study of physics." As if the more he learned, the more he figured out, the more he realized there was to figure out. May I encourage all of my salespeople to encourage their clients to use the format, "I'm engaged." What are you engaged in? I am engaged in the study of financial matters. I'm engaged in the study of cash flow. When you're engaged in the study of something, it forces you to start thinking that you are a student. You are an eternal student.

Let's go back to the class. The class is not for beginners or for experienced people. It's for both. There's something there for everyone. I don't want anybody coming and thinking that it's just a beginner's class, because there are some really important and exciting techniques. A lot of people may not need some of these more powerful techniques, but they need to learn them so that when they are ready, they know about them.

From time to time, I'm going to go ahead and give you a list of different proofs of returns. A lot of these will be one-day trades. Get in, get out, make some money. We've had so much fun with this whole thing because it built up so much income. First of all, your stockbrokers are not going to believe this. When people are calling on the phone and asking, "Well, where do I get a good stockbroker," that's one of the things we teach at the Wall Street Workshop™. The reason that we put these proofs of returns out is so people can go to their stockbrokers if they doubt us and ask, "Could these guys have really on this day bought these options at this price, and sold them on this date?" We make this part of the public record to show people that we mean business.

One of the things that I've taught in my real estate seminars and a lot of my other financial seminars, is that wealth comes from chaos.

You want to create more activity. In my real estate days, I didn't want to be looking at one house. I wanted to create about 15 people calling me trying to sell me their house so I could pick and choose the best one out of the 15. I created more activity in my life than I could possibly do. That's what we want to do at the Wall Street Workshop™.

The next point is that I put all the emphasis on getting out of things–on exit strategies. While everybody else is teaching people how to buy, I want to teach people how to sell and how to get out. That is a little bit fearful to some people, but the class is about getting rid of fear. I'm not going to turn this into a motivational seminar, but I've got to tell you a story about this one man.

I was doing a Wall Street Workshop™ in Seattle, and there was a man in the hallway. He must have been 72 or 73 years old. He came up to me after getting off of the phone and he said, "Wade, what if you're so darn scared, so afraid, that you just can't do anything?"

I just looked at him and said, "What are you not afraid of?" I usually don't come up with great answers, but this was a great thing. It stopped him dead in his tracks.

He said, "What do you mean?"

I said, "Well, what if you lost $20,000?"

He said, "Well, that's about how much I have to start investing."

I said, "Well, if you lost the whole $20,000, would that be a bad thing?"

He said, "I couldn't do that, I would lose everything. I would lose my retirement, everything."

I said, "Well, would you hate to lose $10,000?"

"Yes, I don't want to lose $10,000."

"Well, what about $5,000, what about $2,500?"

"Well, $2,500 wouldn't be so bad."

"Well, what about $1,000?"

"I still don't even want to lose $1,000."

"Okay, well what about $500, $700 or $800?"

He goes, "Yes, I wouldn't mind losing that."

"So there you go. You're not afraid of losing $700, so go and invest that much money. If that's what you're not afraid of, then get started by investing that much money." See, everything's relative.

I'm going to get back to a couple more statements by the salesmen. We don't have too many more, but they are kind of fun. The next one says, "It will free up time to do more important things than make money." I agree. It's spending time with your family. It is spending time with your church and being able to do more with your money, to do those really fun things in life. Churches are built with a lot of faith, but they're also built with a lot of cash.

The next one says, "You'll be taught by those who are successful in the market." These are hand-trained, hand-picked instructors that are there to help you make deals. The best way they can help you make deals is if they are doing the deals themselves. I've got to tell you, most of our seminar speakers and workshop instructors are really exciting, but even if they were boring once in awhile, wouldn't you rather listen to somebody who's boring and really knowledgeable than somebody who's really exciting but doesn't know anything? Luckily, we've been able to blend both.

The next comment was, "You will learn how to be able to depend upon yourself for your personal cash flow." Isn't that what this country is all about, depending on yourself, not some government agency? Rugged individualism, the individual identity that we have and the desire we have to support, to grow, and to build things. If you've built up your cash flow enough so that you have your bills paid, isn't that the fun part about this? You can get money generated by your new cash flow paying your bills, instead of your continual hard work paying your bills. You get your profits from your investments supporting you and helping you buy a new car. You let your cash work for you as hard as you are working for yourself.

Here's the point. Everybody's heard the term "income-producing asset," but for most people who call in, they are their only income-producing asset. If they don't go to work, if their asset doesn't show up to work, there's no income. We're trying to show people at our seminars a way of building up another, different grouping of assets that will produce the income that they need to live on. Isn't that what it's all about? Assets producing income, getting a small amount of assets producing a huge amount of income. It's income we need. We live in a monthly billing society, it's monthly income that we need to pay the bills and to live the lifestyle that we want.

The next one says, "You will learn how to double some of your money every two and a half to four months." Wow, what a statement! This is one of the statements that we use in our advertisements, and I've got to tell you something about these advertisements. I've been criticized for them, but every time I turn around, my students, my instructors, and I are making that kind of money.

Let me tell you another story. I had a brokerage account at a major New York brokerage firm, one of the two biggies. I'd made 19% one month and 23% another month. They wrote me a letter and said, "We want you to move your account somewhere else." When I got to the bottom of this, they said the bottom line was that they saw my advertisements and they didn't want to be seen as being in collusion with me and in backing up my strategies. Isn't that funny? By the way, that stockbroker just cried over losing the account, and he's now gone to another firm.

The next one is that, "You will learn how to find, work, and talk with a stockbroker." That's what we do, just deal in and deal out. We have the stockbrokers on the phone, and actually do the deals right in class. It is a lot of fun.

"Your ability to research the company's stock and act on that research," is the next one. That's true. We show you how to look up information on companies, how to chart them, how to look at them.

The next one says, "You will live a debt-free lifestyle." Boy, wouldn't that be nice? If every one of our customers calling in could feel what it's like to be out of debt, to operate purely with cash. The only way they are going to do that is to make substantial amounts of money—more than what they've got coming in right now—if they're going to be able to live their current lifestyle, and pay off all their debts. Once they've done that, their whole life changes.

The next comment was, "You'll receive faster and larger returns on your investments." It's what we call a BBQ: Bigger, Better, Quicker returns. Bigger meaning they're larger, better that they keep coming in more often, and quicker that you get to start learning to do these one hour, and two- and three-day trades.

Next, "You'll be able to help your family, friends, and church gain financial freedom." That's pretty interesting that they say "church." I know about three or four different churches that have set up little foundations and little corporations, and they have some of their people investing, and are supporting their whole missionary program down in South Africa, or South America. All that from the profits that they are making from their investments.

The next one says, "You'll learn how to successfully steward your assets." That word "steward" means being responsible, almost like a shepherd. I think it's so true. I think we do have an obligation. I've often felt that if there's anything that we can do in our company, it's helping people not only make money, but then to use that money to enhance and better the lives of other people around them.

The next two kind of go hand in hand. I'll read both of them, then I'll make comments on them. "You can walk out of this seminar with more money than when you arrived," and, "You can actually have the workshop paid for by what you did while you were there." Both of these are true. That doesn't happen with everyone. Some classes, it's 20 to 40%, some it's even 50 or 60%. Every class takes on its own personality. I know it's cliché, but people get out of the Wall Street Workshop™ what they put into it. Everybody has their own personality and that's what they bring to the class.

The next comment was, "You can develop it into a business that will allow you to work at home and have more time with your family." We've covered that enough, but the word "business" strikes me. This is a great part-time business. You can do this in your back bedroom; you don't need a lot of money to get started. What money you do have, like $5,000, put that into a brokerage account and get a $5,000 line of credit if you do a margin account. You don't have all the traditional expenses and headaches of a typical business. Here, you can just quit whenever you want. You can make all kinds of money with this business to move and help support your other businesses or other things that you really want to do in life. Treat the stock market like a business, to buy wholesale, sell retail; get in, get out, make money.

The next one says, "The Wall Street Workshop™ is a bridge between where you are and where you want to be." It definitely is. I can't even begin to count all the letters and testimonials that come in saying that people are now able to do so much more with their lives than what they were doing before. It is a bridge, and you look at this big chasm between where people are and where people want to be and you say, "How are you going to get there?" We have a bridge now. Here's where you are, here's where you want to be. We've got a pathway, a bridge if you will, that will help you get there.

The next one says, "You will overcome the fear factor." We've already dealt with that one. The basic way to overcome fear is knowledge. It's the proper application of knowledge, which is wisdom. Think of how fear is serving you. If a fearful thing is not serving you very well, you better learn how to get around it, do away with it, or whatever.

The next one says, "You will learn how to find the news pertaining to stocks and where to find it." Yes, we do that all through the course.

The next one says, "It's fun." It is. A lot of people say, "These are the best two days I've ever spent in my whole life."

And we say, "Golly, you got married, you went on a honeymoon."

They say, "No, no, no, this is better." Well, it is better. It's a really wild experience for some people to come and learn how to make money.

Another comment by one of our in-house sales people says, "The education allows you to make as much money as you want on your own. Lack of education leaves you where you are." I couldn't say it better. Opportunity keeps knocking. Opportunity doesn't knock once, like the old adage says. It keeps knocking. We want to show people how to take advantage of those things.

"Your future transactions can be done anywhere, from a sunny beach, high in the mountains, or sitting on the couch at home." That's true.

The next one says, "An education lasts a lifetime." That is so true. Derek Bock, who, when he said this was the Dean of the Harvard Law School said, "If you think education is expensive, try ignorance." That is so true. If you get this kind of education, it will truly last for a lifetime.

The next one says, "The profits you make from what you learn will remain with you." Not only will the profits remain, they'll be in other investments, but we don't get anything out of what you do. We'll charge a fee for teaching these seminars and we'll teach the strategies, but people get to keep everything that they make. After us, everybody else that has anything to do with them will get something out of what they do—a commission here, a percentage there—but not us. We're the only people in their lives that get nothing out of what they do.

The next comment said, "You will develop a technique that if utilized, will allow you to become financially independent in a relatively short time." Now, it says "technique" that's singular. I keep talking about all these plurals: techniques, strategies. What most people do is pick one that they like and get to be an expert at that one thing. Sometimes two of them, but usually it's just one.

The next comment says, "You'll receive current stock market information." It is so true. If you're talking to a total novice on the phone, tell them about the Wall Street Workshop™ video set. After they come to the Wall Street Workshop™, call them back and congratulate them, thank them for coming, but also tell them about the Next Step™ video training program, and the Next Step™ live seminar because we want to get people more information and better information. We're constantly developing new products to help people make more money and then keep more of what they're making.

What people don't need is to come and spend another two or three days for some namby-pamby, wishy-washy information. What people don't need is another set of tapes and books sitting on their shelves at home collecting dust. What people need is the information and knowledge from books, tapes, and live seminars, to get results—to make a difference in their lives.

The next one says, "You can earn enough to retire yourself and your parents." Let me tell you about Big John. A guy about 6'8" came up to me at a seminar, shaking my hand so hard it literally took me five minutes to have my hand quit hurting. He said his Mom was 78 years old. She had never had anything in her whole life. He went to the Wall Street Workshop™ about six months before and was able to give her a little over $2,000 a month for the last seven months to help her retire better. She was flabbergasted by this amount of money. She had never had this kind of money. It didn't matter how much it was, whether it was $200 or $2,000, but to him, the $2,000 a month to let his Mom retire at a really nice lifestyle, it just did his heart good. He was making about $6,800 to $8,400 a month, but $2,000 every month went to his mom.

You can make money or you can make excuses, but you can't make both.

The next one says this, "With the help of this education, you can have all your needs met while you live on 10% of your income, instead of 90%." Wow! Think this one through. I love this comment. Most people right now are living on 90 to 100%. I did for many years, and now I'm living on about 1% of my income. The cost of feeding my family and taking care of my family is so minuscule compared to the kind of money that I'm making.

The last comment was, "Anybody can do it." I'm not so certain about that. There are a lot of people out there that are just dead between the ears, or that are just not going to learn anything, or be able to change anything, or so fearful that they may not come. But, I guess about 99% of all the people in America could do really well at the Wall Street Workshop™. Not all of them, by any means. So, when people call up and say, "Is this for me, can I benefit from this?" Well, that really is up to them.

I'm just going to make a few more comments. We want to make sure that people stay back to basics. They diversify their portfolios, be wary of the bear market, and be ready to counteract that, especially the bear market mentality that exists. We want people to get a routine and learn. They learn by doing, but we want them to learn a couple of things and just do them over and over again.

The other night I had a chance of going to a Sonics basketball game. Here are these players making $5,000,000 a year, $3,000,000 a year, $2,000,000 a year, and they came out on the floor and started to warm up. I was really watching them and I was so impressed when I saw them doing lay-ups. Doing lay-ups. Here are $5,000,000 a year basketball players doing simple, little, basic lay-ups and chest passes. Back to the basics. To all of you that are a part of my in house sales people, back to the basics. You need to contact people, send out your letters, your cards, and let people know when Wall Street Workshops™ are coming to their area. Get back to the basics yourself. We have a great program, but a lot of people don't know how great it is. Do your lay-ups and get out there and let people know how great this is.

You need to convince people and help people. Rationalize with them, help them see where they are going to be if they don't come to this course? It's the first time anybody's ever put together a course that will cost them more money to stay home than it will ever cost to come. Why are they on the phone? Do they need money to help their kids? Do they need money for a greater retirement? Do they want to give more to their church? How can you, as a salesperson, help somebody know if this course is right for them unless you know where they are and where they want to be? We want to make sure that we're teaching achievable, measurable, and reportable results that people can actually see, feel, and touch. Our job is not to see how much education we can put into people, but to see how much we can get out of them.

All I ask of my salespeople is that you be kind and polite on the phone to people, and that you answer the questions as honestly as you can. We don't want people thinking that the Wall Street Workshop™ is something that it's not. People will get out of it what they put into it. We teach a great course, but people need to come prepared, ready to do the deals, ready to learn. Again, thanks for listening.

Right now there are people sitting there, worrying about their retirement when they could be living it if they knew how to put your strategies to work. They've got assets, they just need to call 1-800-872-7411 and get started. With our guarantee, (within three months of your workshop, we will document three trades that, within one year, will produce a 300% return, or your money back), what have you got to lose?

AVAILABLE RESOURCES

The following books, videos, and audiocassettes have been reviewed by the Stock Market Institute of Learning, Inc.™, Lighthouse Publishing Group, Inc., or Gold Leaf Press staff and are suggested as reading and resource material for continuing education to help with your financial planning, and real estate and stock market investments. Because new ideas and techniques come along and laws change, we're always updating our catalog.

To order a copy of our current catalog, please write or call us at:

Stock Market Institute of Learning, Inc.™
14675 Interurban Avenue South
Seattle, Washington 98168-4664
1-800-872-7411

Or, visit us on our web sites at:
www.wadecook.com
www.lighthousebooks.com

Also, we would love to hear your comments on our products and services, as well as your testimonials on how these products have benefited you. We look forward to hearing from you!

AUDIOCASSETTES/CDs

13 FANTASTIC INCOME FORMULAS-A FREE COMPACT DISC
Presented by Wade B. Cook
Learn 13 cash flow formulas, some of which are taught in the Wall Street Workshop™. Learn to double some of your money in 2 ¹/2 to 4 months.

ZERO TO ZILLIONS™
Presented by Wade B. Cook
A four-album, 16-cassette, powerful audio workshop on Wall Street-understanding the stock market game, playing it successfully, and retiring rich. Learn 11 powerful investment strategies to avoid pitfalls and losses. Learn to catch "day-trippers," how to "bottom fish," write covered calls, and to possibly double your money in one week on options on stock split companies. Wade "Meter Drop" Cook can teach you how he makes fantastic annual returns in his account. You then will have the information to try to follow suit. Each album comes with a workbook, and the entire workshop includes a free bonus video called "Dynamic Dollars," 90 minutes of instruction on how all the strategies can be integrated, giving actual examples of what kinds of returns are possible so you can get in there and play the market successfully. A must for every savvy, would-be investor.

POWER OF NEVADA CORPORATIONS-A FREE CASSETTE
Presented by Wade B. Cook
Nevada Corporations have secrecy, privacy, minimal taxes, no reciprocity with the IRS, and protection for shareholders, officers, and directors. This is a powerful seminar.

INCOME STREAMS-A FREE CASSETTE
Presented by Wade B. Cook
Learn to buy and sell real estate the Wade Cook way. This informative cassette will instruct you in building and operating your own real estate money machine.

24 KARAT
Presented by Wade B. Cook
Learn how to protect your family's finances through anything–including Y2K! 24 Karat seminar on cassette teaches people how currency fluctuates and the safest currency to have. This seminar is packed with must-know information about your future.

THE FINANCIAL FORTRESS HOME STUDY COURSE
Presented by Wade B. Cook

This eight-part series is the last word in entity structuring. It goes far beyond mere financial planning or estate planning. It helps you structure your business and your affairs so that you can avoid the majority of taxes, retire rich, escape lawsuits, bequeath your assets to your heirs without government interference, and, in short-bomb proof your entire estate. There are six audio-cassette seminars on tape, an entity structuring video, and a full kit of documents.

RED LIGHT, GREEN LIGHT™
Presented by Wade B. Cook

This is the ultimate on making timely trades. As CEO of a publicly traded company, Wade Cook discovered a quarterly pattern of stock price behavior that corresponds with corporate new reports. Since most companies file their reports about the same time, many stocks would move accordingly.

If you're playing options, those price movements—or lack thereof—have a dramatic effect on your returns. The Red Light, Green Light course shows you how to recognize and use this information to make more money and avoid losing trades. This "news–no news" discovery is exhilarating!

BOOKS

WALL STREET MONEY MACHINE, VOLUME 1
By Wade B. Cook

The revised and updated version of the book which appeared on the New York Times Business Best-Seller list for over two years, *Wall Street Money Machine, Volume 1* contains the best strategies for wealth enhancement and cash flow creation you'll find anywhere. Throughout this book, Wade Cook describes many of his favorite strategies for generating cash flow through the stock market: rolling stocks, proxy investing, covered calls, and many more. It's a great introduction for creating wealth using the Wade Cook formulas.

WALL STREET MONEY MACHINE, VOLUME 3: BULLS & BEARS (FORMERLY TITLED BEAR MARKET BALONEY)
By Wade B. Cook

A timelier book wouldn't be possible. Wade's predictions came true while the book was at press! Don't miss this insightful look into what makes bull and bear markets and how to make exponential returns in any market.

WALL STREET MONEY MACHINE, VOLUME 4:SAFETY 1ˢᵀ INVESTING
By Wade B. Cook

Over two decades of research and experience have culminated in Wade Cook's book, *Safety 1st Investing*. In it you will learn how to "preserve and grow your asset base as you build an ever-increasing income stream," by utilizing cash flow strategies designed for low risk with good cash flow, including: writing in-the-money calls, bull call spreads, bull put spreads, index plays, and index spreads.

ON TRACK INVESTING
By David R. Hebert

On Track Investing is the instruction book for novice stock market investors or anyone wanting to practice investment strategies without risking actual cash. Combined with your personal game plan, the Simutrade™ System helps you originate good trades, perfect your timing, and check your open trades against your personal criteria. There are Simutrade™ Worksheets and step by step guides for 10 strategies. *On Track Investing* helps you develop a step by step map of what exactly you're going to do and how you're going to accomplish it.

ROLLING STOCKS
By Gregory Witt

Rolling Stocks shows you the simplest and most powerful strategy for profiting from the ups and downs of the stock market. You'll learn how to find rolling stocks, get in smoothly at the right price, and time your exit. You will recognize the patterns of rolling stocks and how to make the most money from these strategies. Apply rolling stocks principles to improve your trading options and fortify your portfolio.

SLEEPING LIKE A BABY
By John C. Hudelson

Perhaps the most predominant reason people don't invest in the stock market is fear. *Sleeping Like A Baby* removes the fear from investing and gives you the confidence and knowledge to invest wisely, safely, and profitably.

You'll learn how to build a high quality portfolio and plan for your future and let your investments follow. Begin to invest as early as possible, and use proper asset allocation and diversification to reduce risk.

MAKING A LIVING IN THE STOCK MARKET

By Bob Eldridge

In simplistic, easy to understand terms and presentation, Bob Eldridge will show you how you can change your job and your life by *Making A Living In The Stock Market*. This powerful book is full of real life examples of profitable trades. Pages full of charts, diagrams, and tables help the reader understand how these strategies are implemented.

If you live for your job, have little or no money at the end of each paycheck, and have forgotten your dreams in days gone past, this book is for you. In *Making A Living In The Stock Market*, you can learn how to make money with cash generating strategies including: channeling stock prices, covered calls, selling naked puts, selling naked calls, call (debit) spread, and stock splits.

101 WAYS TO BUY REAL ESTATE WITHOUT CASH

By Wade B. Cook

Wade Cook has personally achieved success after success in real estate. Now, *101 Ways To Buy Real Estate Without Cash* fills the gap left by other authors who have given all the ingredients but not the whole recipe for real estate investing. This is the book for the investor who wants innovative and practical methods for buying real estate with little or no money down.

COOK'S BOOK ON CREATIVE REAL ESTATE

By Wade B. Cook

Make your real estate buying experiences profitable and fun. *Cook's Book On Creative Real Estate* will show you how! You will learn suggestions for finding the right properties, buying them quickly, and profiting ever quicker.

HOW TO PICK UP FORECLOSURES

By Wade B. Cook

Do you want to become an expert moneymaker in real estate? This book will show you how to buy real estate at 60¢ on the dollar or less. You'll learn to find the house before the auction and purchase it with no bank financing-the easy way to millions in real estate. The market for foreclosures is a tremendous place to learn and prosper. *How To Pick Up Foreclosures* takes Wade's methods from Real Estate Money Machine and super charges them by applying the fantastic principles to already-discounted properties.

OWNER FINANCING

By Wade B. Cook

This is a short but invaluable booklet you can give to sellers who hesitate to sell you their property using the owner financing method. Let this pamphlet convince both you and them. The special report, "Why Sellers Should Take Monthly Payments," is included for free!

REAL ESTATE FOR REAL PEOPLE
By Wade B. Cook

A priceless, comprehensive overview of real estate investing, this book teaches you how to buy the right property for the right price, at the right time. Wade Cook explains all of the strategies you'll need, and gives you 20 reasons why you should start investing in real estate today. Learn how to retire rich with real estate, and have fun doing it.

REAL ESTATE MONEY MACHINE
By Wade B. Cook

Wade's first best-selling book reveals the secrets of Wade Cook's own system–the system he earned his first million from. This book teaches you how to make money regardless of the state of the economy. Wade's innovative concepts for investing in real estate not only avoids high interest rates, but avoids banks altogether.

BLUEPRINTS FOR SUCCESS, VOLUME 1
Contributors: Wade Cook, Debbie Losse, Joel Black, Dan Wagner, Tim Semingson, Rich Simmons, Greg Witt, JJ Childers, Keven Hart, Dave Wagner and Steve Wirrick

Blueprints For Success, Volume 1 is a compilation of chapters on building your wealth through your business and making your business function successfully. The chapters cover: education and information gathering, choosing the best business for you from all the different types of business, and a variety of other skills necessary for becoming successful. Your business can't afford to miss out on these powerful insights!

BRILLIANT DEDUCTIONS
By Wade B. Cook

Do you want to make the most of the money you earn? Do you want to have solid tax havens and ways to reduce the taxes you pay? This book is for you! Learn how to get rich in spite of the updated tax laws. See new tax credits, year-end maneuvers, and methods for transferring and controlling your entities. Learn to structure yourself and your family for tax savings and liability protection.

MILLION HEIRS
By John V. Childers, Jr.

In his reader-friendly style, attorney John V. Childers, Jr. explains how you can prepare your loved ones for when you pass away. He explains many details you need to take care of right away, before a death occurs, as well as strategies for your heirs to utilize. Don't leave your loved ones unprepared– get *Millions Heirs.*

THE SECRET MILLIONAIRE GUIDE TO NEVADA CORPORATIONS
By John V. Childers, Jr.

What does it mean to be a secret millionaire? In *The Secret Millionaire Guide To Nevada Corporations,* attorney John V. Childers, Jr. outlines exactly how you can use some of the secret, extraordinary business tactics used by many of today's super-wealthy to protect your assets from the ravages of lawsuits and other destroyers using Nevada Corporations. You'll understand why the state of Nevada has become the preferred jurisdiction for those desiring to establish corporations and how to utilize Nevada Corporations for your financial benefit.

WEALTH 101
By Wade B. Cook

This incredible book brings you 101 strategies for wealth creation and protection that you can't afford to miss. Front to back, it is packed full of tips and tricks to supercharge your financial health. If you need to generate more cash flow, this book shows you how through several various avenues. If you are already wealthy, this is the book that will show you strategy upon strategy for decreasing your tax liability and increasing your peace of mind through liability protection.

A+
By Wade B. Cook

A+ is a collection of wisdom, thoughts, and principles of success, which can help you, make millions, even billions of dollars and live an A+ life. As you will see, Wade Cook consistently tries to live his life "in the second mile," to do more than asked, to be above normal.

If you want to live a successful life, you need great role models to follow. For years, Wade Cook's life has been a quest to find successful characteristics of his role models and implement them in his own life. In *A+,* Wade will encourage you to find and incorporate the most successful principles and characteristics of success in your life, too. Don't spend another day living less than an A+ life!

BUSINESS BUY THE BIBLE

By Wade B. Cook

Inspired by the Creator, the Bible truly is the authority for running the business of life. Throughout *Business Buy The Bible*, you are provided with practical advice that helps you apply God's word to your life. You'll learn how you can apply God's word to your life. You'll learn how you can apply God's words to saving, spending and investing, and how you can control debt instead of being controlled by it. You'll also learn how to use God's principles in your daily business activities and prosper.

DON'T SET GOALS (THE OLD WAY)

By Wade B. Cook

Don't Set Goals (The Old Way) will teach you to be a goal-getter, not just a goal-setter. You'll learn that achieving goals is the result of prioritizing and acting. *Don't Set Goals (The Old Way)* shows you how taking action and "paying the price" is more important than simply making the decision to do something. Don't just set goals. Go out and get your goals, go where you want to go!

WADE COOK'S POWER QUOTES, VOLUME 1

By Wade B. Cook

Wade Cook's Power Quotes, Volume 1 is chock full of exciting quotes that have motivated and inspired Mr. Cook. Wade Cook continually asks his students, "To whom are you listening?" He knows that if you get your advice and inspiration from successful people, you'll become successful yourself. He compiled *Wade Cook's Power Quotes, Volume 1* to provide you with a millionaire-on-call when you need advice.

LIVING IN COLOR

By Renae Knapp

Renae Knapp is the leading authority on the Blue Base/Yellow Base Color System and is recognized worldwide for her research and contribution to the study of color. Industries, universities, and men and women around the globe use Renae's tried and true-scientifically proven-system to achieve measurable results.

In *Living In Color*, Renae Knapp teaches you easy to understand methods, which empower you to get more from your life by harnessing the power of color. In an engaging, straightforward way, Renae Knapp teaches the scientific Blue Base/Yellow Base Color System and how to achieve harmony and peace using color. You will develop a mastery of color harmony and an awareness of the amazing role color plays in every area of your life.

Y2K GOLD RUSH
By Wade B. Cook

This book is about how to invest in gold. By reading *Y2K Gold Rush*, you will understand the historical importance of gold. You will learn about the ownership of gold coins and gold stocks, and the benefits of both. You will see that adding gold to your investment portfolio will diversify your assets, safeguard you and your family against catastrophe, and add excitement and profits.

VIDEOS

DYNAMIC DOLLARS VIDEO
By Wade B. Cook

Wade Cook's 90-minute introduction to the basics of his Wall Street formulas and strategies. In this presentation designed especially for video, Wade explains the meter drop philosophy, rolling stocks, basics of proxy investing, and writing covered calls. Perfect for anyone looking for a little basic information.

THE WALL STREET WORKSHOP™ VIDEO SERIES
By Wade B. Cook

If you can't make it to the Wall Street Workshop™ soon, get a head start with these videos. Ten albums containing 11 hours of intense instruction on rolling stocks, options on stock split companies, writing covered calls, and eight other tested and proven strategies designed to help you increase the value of your investments. By learning, reviewing, and implementing the strategies taught here, you will gain the knowledge and the confidence to take control of your investments, and get your money to work hard for you.

THE NEXT STEP VIDEO SERIES
By Team Wall Street

The advanced version of the Wall Street Workshop™. Full of power-packed strategies from Wade Cook, this is not a duplicate of the Wall Street Workshop™, but a very important partner. The methods taught in this seminar will supercharge the strategies taught in the Wall Street Workshop™ and teach you even more ways to make more money!

In The Next Step, you'll learn how to find the stocks to fit the formulas through technical analysis, fundamentals, home trading tools, and more.

BUILD PERPETUAL INCOME (BPI)-A VIDEOCASSETTE

Wade Cook Seminars, Inc. is proud to present Build Perpetual Income, the latest in our ever-expanding series of seminar home study courses. In this video, you will learn powerful real estate cash-flow generating techniques, such as: power negotiating strategies, buying and selling mortgages, writing contracts, finding and buying discount properties, and avoiding debt.

SPREAD & BUTTER™

Spread & Butter™ is Wade Cook's tremendously popular one-day semi-nar on video. Created in early 1999, this home study course is a live taping of Wade himself teaching his favorite cash flow spread strategies. You will learn everything, from basic Bull Put and Bull Call Spreads to Index Spreads and Calendar Spreads, and how to use each effectively.

CLASSES OFFERED

WEALTH U™

Wealth U™ combines the most powerful, practical and pragmatic train-ing and tools available from Stock Market Institute of Learning, Inc.™, a com-pany that produces more than 30 powerful and effective live and home-study courses. Our education can and does change people's lives, but we have dis-covered that often newer students are unsure what classes they need most in order to gain the skills necessary for creating, building and protecting net worth.

Wealth U™ is the answer: a comprehensive yet flexible program of core courses, services and tools rolled into one cost-effective package. Wealth U™ is based on a two-fold vision of financial freedom. The key to this vision is in understanding both how to increase income and assets and then how to pro-tect that wealth from the challenges of our economic system. Wealth U™ includes everything you need in order to learn, practice and successfully imple-ment our wealth strategies and reach your dreams!

The first goal is to train our students how to amass enough income-producing assets to comfortably support their chosen lifestyle. Wealth U™ courses look at the complexities of the market from several different angles and provide attendees with strategies to help them make educated and prof-itable trading decisions. Our market strategies can net substantial gains for the student who is willing to study and apply them. Wealth U™ also includes tools to support our students, from home-study courses for review, to an on-line resource for "watching over the shoulders" of professional traders as they implement our strategies in real trade situations.

Our second goal is to help students understand the vehicles available for protecting their assets and income. With diligent practice and careful planning, trading can become your business. To protect the profits of this new business, Wealth U™'s business classes help students learn to build a new way of life using legal entities such as Nevada corporations, trusts, limited partnerships and more. Wealth U™ students learn how to protect their assets from frivolous lawsuits and excessive taxation.

If you want to be wealthy, this is the place to be.

THE WALL STREET WORKSHOP™
Presented by Wade B. Cook and Team Wall Street
The Wall Street Workshop™ teaches you how to make incredible money in all markets. It teaches you the tried-and-true strategies that have made hundreds of people wealthy.

THE NEXT STEP WORKSHOP
Presented by Wade B. Cook and Team Wall Street
An advanced Wall Street Workshop designed to help those ready to take their trading to the next level and treat it as a business. This seminar is open only to graduates of the Wall Street Workshop™.

YOUTH WALL STREET WORKSHOP
Presented by Team Wall Street
Wade Cook has made a personal commitment to empower the youth of today with desire and knowledge to be self-sufficient. Now you, too, can make a personal commitment to your youth by sending them to the Youth Wall Street Workshop and start your own family dynasty in the process!

Our Youth Wall Street Workshop teaches the power and money making potential of the stock market strategies of the Wall Street Workshop™. The pace is geared to the students, with more time devoted to vocabulary, principles and concepts that may be new to them.

Your children and grandchildren can learn these easy to understand strategies and get that "head start" in life!

If you're considering the Wall Street Workshop™ for the first time, take advantage of our free Youth Wall Street Workshop promotion and bring a son, daughter, or grandchild with you (ages 13 to 18, student, living at home).

Help make your children financially secure in the future by giving them the helping hand in life we all wish we had received.

FINANCIAL CLINIC
Presented by Wade Cook and Team Wall Street

People from all over are making money, lots of money, in the stock market using the proven bread and butter strategies taught by Wade Cook. Is trading in the stock market for you?

Please accept our invitation to come hear for yourself about the amazing money-making strategies we teach. Our Financial Clinic is designed to help you understand how you can learn these proven stock market strategies. In three short hours you will be introduced to some of the 11 proven strategies we teach at the Wall Street Workshop™. Discover for yourself how they work and how you can use them in your life to get the things you want for you and your family. Come to this introductory event and see what we have to offer. Then make the decision yourself!

THE ONE-MINUTE COMMUTE (TRADING AT HOME)
Presented by Keven Hart

This one-day clinic will take you from being a semi-active investor to trading on a daily basis, giving you the freedom to dictate your own schedule and move forward on your own predetermined timeline. Trade from home and stay close to your family. This condensed training will get you where you want to go by helping you practice trading as a business, showing you which resources produce wealth through crucial and timely information, selecting appropriate strategies, qualifying your trades and helping you time both entries and exits.

EXECUTIVE RETREAT
Presented by Wade B. Cook and Team Wall Street

Created especially for the individuals already owning or planning to establish Nevada Corporations, the Executive Retreat is a unique opportunity for corporate executives to participate in workshops geared toward streamlining operations and maximizing efficiency and impact.

WEALTH INSTITUTE
Presented by Wade B. Cook and Team Wall Street

This three-day workshop defines the art of asset protection and entity planning. During these three days we will discuss, in depth and detail, the six domestic entities which will protect you from lawsuits, taxes, or other financial losses, and help you retire rich.

BUSINESS ENTITY SKILLS TRAINING (B.E.S.T.™)
Presented by Wade B. Cook and Team Wall Street

Learn about the six powerful entities you can use to protect your wealth and your family. Learn the secrets of asset protection, eliminate your fear of litigation, and minimize your taxes.

SUPPORT

SUPPORT is designed to be a one-year continuing education program with six one-day events focused on enhancing your knowledge is specific areas. One of the keys to successful trading is to find a strategy and system that fits your personality, available time, money resources, and risk tolerance. There's no better way to design and implement a personal system than to study several until you identify the one that clicks with your lifestyle and trading goals.

SUPPORT is designed as continuing education for graduates of the Wall Street Workshop™ and others who are interested in specialized training in specific strategies. Students can purchase SUPPORT classes separately or pay a low package price for the right the attend multiple classes of your choosing. Focus on one or two favorite strategies or instructors, or explore several to find the right style for your personality and goals!

ASSORTED RESOURCES

WEALTH INFORMATION NETWORK™ (W.I.N.™)

This subscription Internet service provides you with the latest financial formulas and updated entity structuring strategies. New, timely information is entered Monday through Friday, sometimes four or five times a day. Wade Cook and his Team Wall Street staff write for W.I.N.™, giving you updates on their own current stock plays, companies who announced earnings, companies who announced stock splits, and the latest trends in the market.

W.I.N.™ is also divided into categories according to specific strategies and contains archives of all our trades so you can view our history. If you are just getting started in the stock market, this is a great way to follow people who are doubling their money every $2^1/2$ to 4 months. If you are experienced already, it's the way to confirm your feelings and research with others who are generating wealth through the stock market.

IQ PAGER™

This is a system which beeps you as events and announcements are made on Wall Street. With IQ Pager™, you'll receive information about events like major stock split announcements, earnings surprises, important mergers and acquisitions, judgements or court decisions involving big companies, important bankruptcy announcements, big winners and losers, and disasters. If you're getting your financial information from the evening news, you're getting it too late. The key to the stock market is timing. Especially when you're trading in options, you need up-to-the-minute (or second) information. You cannot afford to sit at a computer all day looking for news or wait for your broker to call. IQ Pager™ is the ideal partner to the Wealth Information Network™ (W.I.N.™).

The Incorporation Handbook
By Wade B. Cook

Incorporation made easy! This handbook tells you who, why, and, most importantly, how to incorporate. Included are samples of the forms you will use when you incorporate, as well as a step-by-step guide from the experts.

Travel Agent Information
By John Childers and Wade Cook

The only sensible solution for the frequent traveler. This kit includes all of the information and training you need to be an outside travel agent for a stable company. There are no hassles, no requirements, no forms or restrictions, just all the benefits of traveling for substantially less every time.

Explanations Newsletter

In the wild and crazy stock market game, *EXPLANATIONS* Newsletter will keep you on your toes! Every month you'll receive coaching, instruction and encouragement with engaging articles designed to bring your trading skills to a higher level. Learn new twists on Wade's 11 basic strategies, find out about beneficial research tools, read reviews on the latest investment products and services, and get detailed answers to your trading questions. With *EXPLANATIONS*, you'll learn to be your own best asset in the stock market game and stay on track to a rapidly growing portfolio! Continue your education as an investor and subscribe today!

GLOSSARY

ASK - The current price for which a security may be bought (purchased).

AT THE CLOSE - The last price for which a stock security trades for, when the market closes trading for the day.

AT THE OPEN - The first price for which a stock security trades, when the market opens trading for the day.

BID - The current price at which the stock trades.

BUYING A HEDGE - The purchase of future options as a means of protecting against an increase or decrease in the price of a security in the future.

BUYING POWER - The dollar amount of securities that a client can purchase using only the special memorandum account balance and without depositing any additional equity.

CALL - An option contract giving the owner the right (but not the obligation) to buy 100 shares of stock at a strike price on or before the expiration date.

CALL PRICE - The price paid (usually a premium over the par value of the issue) for stocks or bonds redeemed prior to maturity of the issue.

CALL SPREAD - The result of an investor buying a call on a particular security and writing a call with a different expiration date, different exercise price, or both, on the same security.

CASH AMOUNT - An account in which a client is required to pay in full for securities purchased within a specific amount of time from the trade date.

COVER - 1) Future options purchased to offset a short position. 2) Being "long actuals" when shorting futures.

COVERED CALL WRITER - An investor who writes a call and owns some other asset that guarantees the ability to perform if the call is exercised.

HEDGE - A securities transaction that reduces the risk on an existing investment position.

IN THE MONEY - A call option is said to be in-the-money if the current market value of the underlying interest is above the exercise price of the option. A put option is said to be in-the-money if the current market value of the underlying interest is below the exercise price of the option.

INITIAL MARGIN REQUIREMENT - The amount of equity a customer must deposit when making a new purchase in a margin account.

INITIAL PUBLIC OFFERING (IPO) - A company's initial public offering, sometimes referred to as "going public," is the first sale of stock by the company to the public.

INTRINSIC VALUE - The amount, if any, by which an option is in-the-money.

LONG - (1) Referring to a person's position as the writer of an option. (2) Owning the security on which an option is written.

LONG STRADDLE - The act of buying a call and a put on a stock with the same strike price and expiration date.

LONG-TERM EQUITY ANTICIPATION SECURITIES (LEAPS®) - An option with an extended expiration date.

MARGIN - Effectively, a loan from the broker, allowing the investor to purchase securities of a greater value than the actual cash available in the account.

MARGIN ACCOUNT - An account in which a brokerage firm lends a client part of the purchase price of securities.

MARKET MAKER - A dealer willing to accept the risk of holding securities in order to facilitate trading in a particular security or securities.

MARKET VALUE -The price at which an investor will buy or sell each share of common stock or each bond at a given time.

MARRIED PUT - When an investor buys a stock and on the same day buys a put on that stock and specifically identifies that position as a hedge.

MONTHLY INCOME PREFERRED SECURITIES (MIPS) - Preferred stocks that pay monthly dividends.

NEWS DRIVEN - Referring to the volatility in the movement of a particular stock being affected by news, not by any intrinsic value to the company.

OPTION - The right to buy (or sell) a specified amount of a security (stocks, bonds, futures contracts, et cetera) at a specified price on or before a specific date (American style options).

OUT OF THE MONEY - If the exercise price of a call is above the current market value of the underlying interest, or if the exercise price of a put is below the current market value of the underlying interest, the option is said to be out-of-the-money by that amount.

OVER THE COUNTER (OTC) - A security that is not listed or traded on a recognized exchange.

PRICE SPREAD - A spread involving the purchase and sale of two options on the same stock with the same expiration date but with different exercise prices.

PUT - An option contract that gives the owner the right to force the sale of a specified number of shares of stock at a specified price on or before a specific date.

PUT SPREAD - An investment in which an investor purchases one put on a particular stock and sells another put on the same stock but with a different expiration date, exercise price, or both.

RANGE RIDER - A stock that has a repeating pattern of highs and lows on its price range and gradually rises to a higher range over a period of time.

REVERSE RANGE RIDER - A stock that has a repeating pattern of highs and lows on its price range and gradually drops to a low range over a period of time.

REVERSE STOCK SPLIT - An increase in the stock's par value by reducing the number of shares outstanding.

ROLLING STOCK - A stock that fluctuates between its high and low price points for long periods of time and whose history makes it seem to be predictable.

SHORT - A condition resulting from selling an option and not owning the related securities.

SHORT HEDGE - A short securities or actuals position protected by a long call position.

SHORT STRADDLE - The position established by writing a call and a put on the same stock with the same strike price and expiration month.

SPREAD - 1) Consisting of being a buyer and a seller of the same type of option with the options having a different expiration date, exercise price, or both. 2) The difference between the bid and the ask for a stock or option.

STOCK SPLIT - A reduction in the par value of a stock caused by the issuance of additional stock, such as issuing two shorts for one.

STRADDLE - Either a long or a short position in a call and a put on the same security with the same expiration date and exercise price.

STRANGLE - A combination of a put and a call where both options are out-of-the-money. A strangle can be profitable only if the market is highly volatile and makes a major move in either direction.

STRIKE PRICE - The price at which the underlying security will be sold if the option buyer exercises his/her rights in the contract; the agreed-upon sale price; the price you are willing to sell for.

TICKER SYMBOL - A trading symbol used by a company to identify itself on a stock exchange.

TIME VALUE - Whatever the premium of the option is in addition to its intrinsic value.

VOLATILE - When speaking of the stock market and of stocks or securities, this is when the market tends to vary often and wildly in prices.